Duel to the Death

Duel to the Death

Eyewitness Accounts of Great Battles at Sea

Compiled by John Slinkman
and the Editors of *Navy Times*

Illustrated with photographs

Harcourt, Brace & World, Inc., New York

Contents

"The boldest maneuvers are the safest."
—Horatio Lord Nelson

Man is a distinctively aggressive animal. He has fought, we know, ever since recorded time and, unquestionably, long before that. After he learned how to build boats, he discovered he could extend his warrings to the surface of the sea.

More than two thousand years before Christ, the Egyptians and Cretans were putting out in their well-designed, high-prowed craft. A thousand years later, the Phoenicians proved to be such skilled navigators that their very name became synonymous with the oceans.

Not until the fifth century, however, was there a naval clash on the grand scale involving many squadrons of warships and tactical maneuverings. In 480 B.C., a fleet of more than three hundred Greek vessels, including one-hundred-and-twenty-foot-long triremes, sank two hundred vessels of their Persian foe off Salamis.

This mammoth and sanguinary contest not only heralded future sea encounters but also altered the course of history. Greek civilization was enabled to continue, and our cultural legacy from it was assured.

As the centuries rolled by and the world's population kept expanding, the desire as well as the need for international commerce increased in the same tempo and volume. The marine battlefield shifted northward from the Mediterranean, although the old competitive factors, especially the guarding of trade routes, had remained relatively unchanged since the Pharaohs. The Spanish, Portuguese, Dutch, French, English, and even the Danes became maritime contestants at different periods in history.

There were numerous sea battles, but who was to chronicle them? There were neither correspondents nor newspapers to report the ancient engagements, nor readers to be enlightened by the tidings.

Herodotus, who was four years old at the time of Salamis, was—like so many historians then—a storyteller. Aeschylus was, too. Even after the dawn of the printing press, eyewitness, exact reports of the significant historical events were not available to the public, in spite of the diaries and letters accruing from the active pens of educated men and women. An exception was Samuel Pepys, the faithful scribe of the British Admiralty, who left behind him a graphic diary account of the London fire in 1666.

Not until the American Civil War were battles, land and sea, reported in the minute-by-minute "you are there" fashion of today. From that time onward, there is a wealth of detailed and dramatic documentation in the wake of warfare.

Fragmentary and frustrating as they are, the testimonies of John Paul Jones and of Dr. William Beatty, surgeon aboard the Victory, are good examples of narrative reporting at the turn of the nineteenth century. The American naval *immortal was an uneducated man, as his writing clearly reveals. The British doctor reveals himself to be the opposite.*

These accounts, the subjects of the first two chapters, together with the subsequent ones in this volume, are reproduced not as critical analyses of any of the engagements involved but rather in an effort to recapture the mood and spirit and other elusive ingredients of yesterday's naval conflicts, some of which were to have their influence on wars and empires. Others were only angry red flickers against the dark horizon of war, of particular moment to those who were the participants.

"... Only Begun to Fight!"

◆◆◆ *John Paul Jones, the first of America's naval leaders, was only twenty-two years old in 1769 when he guided his first command to sea. She was the coastal sailer* John, *plying the West Indian rum trade.*

It was a tough run, and the ships were appropriately manned by tough crews. Scotland-born, diminutive John Paul (he added the Jones later) followed the harsh maritime tradition of the Royal Navy and East Indiamen and proved an austere master from the start. A ship's carpenter died at sea after a flogging the young captain had ordered.

Although briefly imprisoned in Scotland, Jones was exonerated when he proved to the satisfaction of a court of inquiry that the carpenter had actually succumbed to malaria. In 1773, while at Tobago, a British colony off Venezuela, he ran a mutinous crewman through with his sword.

This was too much. Fellow shippers in port at the time implored him to seek refuge without delay in the United States before the riffraff fraternity of the sea murdered him.

This he did and two years later was sporting a lieutenant's commission in such a ragged navy as the newly independent states could hastily assemble.

At this stage, the Continental Congress was not interested in exploring the background of a trained salt or fighter too deeply. Jones proved instantly successful as a privateer and, in 1778, commanding the Ranger, *raided the coast of his native Scotland. The Earl of Selkirk, a leading peer, was spared kidnaping as hostage only by his absence.*

Shortly afterwards, Captain Jones encountered his first truly formidable adversary, H.M.S. Drake. *He forced the sloop to strike after a bloody engagement. There was not, however, the spirit in Jones's crew or the semihero worship to which Lord Nelson was accustomed. Going into battle, Jones bluntly told his surly, grumbling men that he'd shoot the first one who was dawdling at his gun.*

The next year Jones took command of the Duras, *presented to America by the French. A small, fast vessel of forty guns, with a main battery of 12-pounders, she was renamed the* Bon Homme Richard, *meaning "Good Man Richard," after Benjamin Franklin's publication,* Poor Richard's Almanac. *Aboard his new flagship, the thirty-two-year-old captain led a squadron of small warships with French commanders along the coasts of the British Isles during the last days of August and the first half of September, 1779.*

By the middle of that autumn month, in the preserves of His Brittanic Majesty's navy, Jones had captured seventeen enemy ships—a daring and contemptuous exploit that was wholly in character.

When Jones arrived off Flamborough Head on the east coast of England, on September 23, his command, in addition to his own ship, was comprised of the frigates Alliance *and* Pallas, *a former privateer. Both were commanded and crewed by Frenchmen. In these British waters northeast of Hull, Jones overtook a large Baltic-bound convoy at dusk, escorted by H.M.S.* Serapis, *a glowering frigate studded with 18-pounders along two decks, and the smaller* Countess of Scarborough.

The Bon Homme Richard, *with but a single deck, immediately gave battle to her huge adversary after signaling the* Alliance *to join the attack. Curiously, Pierre Landais, commanding the* Alliance, *stood off, out of range, ignoring Jones's order.*

The following is Jones's account, in his own quaint English, of the engagement: ◆◆◆

When the fleet discovered us bearing down, all the merchant ships crowded sail towards the shore. The two ships of war that protected the fleet, at the same time steered from the land, and made the disposition for the battle. In approaching the enemy I crowded every possible sail, and made the signal for the line of battle, to which the *Alliance* showed no attention.

Earnest as I was for the action, I could not reach the Commodore's ship until seven in the evening, being then within pistol shot. When he hailed the *B.H.R.*, we answered him by firing a whole broadside.

The battle being thus begun, was continued with unremitting fury. Every method was practiced on both sides to gain an advantage, and rake each other; and I must confess that the enemy's ship being much more manageable than the *B.H.R.*, gained thereby several times an advantageous situation, in spite of my best endeavors to prevent it. As I had to deal with an enemy of *greatly superior force*, I was under the necessity of closing with him, to prevent the advantage which he had over me in point of maneuver.

It was my intention to lay the *B.H.R.* athwart the enemy's bow, but as that operation required great dexterity in the management of both sails and helm, and some of our braces being shot away, it did not exactly succeed to my wishes; the enemy's bowsprit, however, came over the *B.H.R.*'s poop by the mizzen mast, and I made both ships fast together in that situation, which by the action of the wind on the enemy's sails, forced her stern close to the *B.H.R.*'s bow, so that the ships lay square alongside of each other, the yards being all entangled, and the cannon of each ship touching the opponent's side.

When this position took place it was eight o'clock, previous to which the *B.H.R.* had received sundry 18-pounds shot below the water, and leaked very much. My battery of 12-pounders, on which I had placed my chief dependence, being commanded by Lieut. Deal [Lieutenant Richard Deal] and Col. Weibert, and manned principally with American seamen and French volunteers, were entirely silenced and abandoned.

As to the six old 18-pounders that formed the battery of the lower gun-deck, they did no service whatever: two out of three of them burst at the first fire, and killed almost all the men who were stationed to manage them. Before this time too, Col. de Chamillard, who commanded a party of twenty soldiers on the poop, had abandoned that station, after having lost some of his men [who deserted]. I had now only two pieces of cannon, 9-pounders, on the quarter deck that were not silenced, and not one of the heavier cannon was fired during the rest of the action.

The purser, Mr. Mease, who commanded the guns on the quarter deck, being dangerously wounded in the head, I was obliged to fill his place, and with great difficulty rallied a few men, and shifted over one of the lee quarter-deck guns, so that we afterward played three pieces of 9-pounders upon the enemy. The tops alone seconded the fire of this little battery, and held out bravely during the whole of the action; especially the main top, where Lieut. Stack commanded. I directed the fire of one of the three cannon against the mainmast, with double-headed shot, while the other two were exceedingly well served with grape and canister shot to silence the enemy's musketry, and clear her decks, which was at last effected. The enemy were, as I have since understood, on the instant of calling for quarters, when the cowardice or treachery of three of my under officers induced them to call to the enemy.

The English commodore asked me if I demanded quarters, and I having answered him in the most determined negative [it was at this moment Jones called, "Struck, sir? I have only begun to fight!"] they renewed the battle with double fury; they were unable to stand the deck, but the fire of their cannon, especially the lower battery, which was entirely formed of 18-pounders, was incessant; both ships were set on fire in various places, and the scene was dreadful beyond the reach of language.

To account for the timidity of my three under officers, I mean the gunner, the carpenter, and the master-at-arms, I must observe that the two first were slightly wounded, and as the ship had received various shots under water, and one of the pumps being shot away, the carpenter expressed his fear that she should sink, and the other two concluded that she was sinking; which occasioned the gunner to run aft on the poop without my knowledge, to strike the colors. Fortunately for me, a cannonball had done that before, by carrying away the ensign staff; he was therefore reduced to the necessity of sinking, as he supposed, or of calling for quarter, and he preferred the latter.

All this time the *B.H.R.* had sustained the action alone, and the enemy, though much superior in force, would have been very glad to have got clear, as appears by their own acknowledgments, and by their having let go on anchor the instant that I laid them on board, by which means they would have escaped had I not made them well fast to the *B.H.R.*

At last, at half past nine o'clock, the *Alliance* appeared, and I now thought the battle was at an end; but, to my utter astonishment, he discharged a broadside full into the stern of the *B.H.R.;* we called to him for God's sake to forbear firing into the *B.H.R.;* yet he passed along the off side of the ship and continued firing.

There was no possibility of his mistaking the enemy's ship for the *B.H.R.*, there being the most essential difference in their appearance and construction; besides, it was then full moonlight, and the sides of the *B.H.R.* were all black, while the sides of the prizes were yellow. Yet, for the greater security, I showed the signal of our reconnaissance, by putting out three lanterns, one at the head [bow], another at the stern [quarter], and the third in the middle, in a horizontal line.

Every tongue cried that he was firing into the wrong ship, but nothing availed; he passed round, firing into the *B.H.R.*'s head, stern, and broadside, and by one of his volleys killed several of my best men, and mortally wounded a good officer on the forecastle. My situation was really deplorable.

The *B.H.R.* received various shot under water from the *Alliance;* the leak gained on the pump, and the fire increased much on board both ships. Some officers persuaded me to strike, of whose courage and good sense I entertain a high opinion.

My treacherous master-at-arms let loose all my prisoners without my knowledge, and my prospect became gloomy indeed. I would not, however, give up the point. The enemy's mainmast began to shake, their firing decreased, ours rather increased, and the British colors were struck at half an hour past ten o'clock.

This prize proved to be the British ship of war the *Serapis,* a new ship of 44 guns, built on their most approved construction, with two complete batteries, one of them of 18-pounders, and commanded by the brave Commodore Richard Pearson. I had yet two enemies to encounter far more formidable than the Britons; I mean fire and water. The *Serapis* was attacked only by the first, but the *B.H.R.* was assailed by both: there was five feet of water in the hold, and though it was moderate from the explosion of so much gunpowder, yet the three pumps that remained could with difficulty only keep the water from gaining.

The fire broke out in various parts of the ship, in spite of all the water that could be thrown to quench it, and at length broke out as low as the powder magazine, and within a few inches of the powder. In that dilemma, I took out the powder upon deck, ready to be thrown overboard at the last extremity, and it was ten o'clock the next day, the twenty-fourth, before the fire was entirely extinguished.

With respect to the situation of the *B.H.R.*, the rudder was cut entirely off, the stern frame and the transoms were almost entirely cut away, the timbers, by the lower deck especially, from the mainmast to the stern, being greatly decayed with age, were mangled beyond my power of description, and a person must have been an eyewitness to form a just idea of the tremendous scene of carnage, wreck, and ruin that everywhere appeared. Humanity cannot but recoil from the prospect of such finished horror, and lament that war should produce such fatal consequences.

After the carpenters, as well as Capt. de Cottineau, and other men of sense, had well examined and surveyed the ship [which was not finished before five in the evening], I found every person to be convinced that it was impossible to keep the *B.H.R.* afloat so as to reach a port if the wind should increase, it being then only a very moderate breeze.

I had but little time to remove my wounded, which now became unavoidable, and which was effected in the course of the night and the next morning. I was determined to keep the *B.H.R.* afloat, and, if possible, to bring her into port. For that purpose, the first lieutenant of the *Pallas* continued on board, with a party of men to attend the pumps, with boats in waiting ready to take them on board, in case the water should gain on them too fast. The wind augmented in the night and the next day, on the twenty-fifth, so that it was impossible to prevent the good old ship from sinking.

They did not abandon her till after nine o'clock; the water was then up to the lower deck; and a little after ten, I saw with inexpressible grief the last glimpse of the *B.H.R.* No lives were lost with the ship, but it was impossible to save the stores of any sort whatever. I lost even the best part of my clothes, books, and papers; and several of my officers lost all their clothes and effects.

Captain [de Brulot] Cottineau engaged the *Countess of Scarborough* and took her after an hour's action, while the *B.H.R.* engaged the *Serapis*. The *Countess of Scarborough* is an armed ship of twenty 6-pounders, and was commanded by a king's officer. In the action, the *Countess of Scarborough* and the *Serapis* were at a considerable distance asunder; and the *Alliance,* as I am informed, fired into the *Pallas* and killed some men. If it should be asked why the convoy was suffered to escape, I must answer, that I was myself in no condition to pursue, and that none of the rest showed any inclination.

The *Alliance,* too, was in a state to pursue the fleet, not having had a single man wounded, or a single shot fired at her from the *Serapis,* and only three that did execution from the *Countess of Scarborough* at such a distance that one stuck in the side, and the other two just touched and then dropped into the water. The *Alliance* killed one man only on board the *Serapis*. As Captain de Cottineau charged himself with manning and securing the prisoners of the *Countess of Scarborough;* I think the escape of the Baltic fleet cannot so well be charged to his account.

I should have mentioned, that the mainmast and mizzentop-mast of the *Serapis* fell overboard soon after the captain had come on board the *B.H.R.*

September, 1779

—*John Paul Jones's Commemoration at Annapolis, April 24, 1906,* Government Printing Office, Washington, 1907 (reprinted, 1966)

♦♦♦ *It was subsequently assumed that Pierre Landais, captain of the* Alliance, *was attacking his own flagship intentionally. Discharged previously from the French Navy, Landais was later court-martialed by the American Navy. His defense counsel, surprisingly perhaps, was Samuel Adams. Landais, crazed with jealousy and ambition, had wished to dispose of the* Bon Homme Richard *and alone enjoy the glory of* Serapis's *surrender. He confessed as much to a friend.*

Trouble proved to be Jones's continuing companion. When, after the Revolution, Congress voted him a medal in lieu of a pension or even an admiral's rank for his services, Jones shopped around for another employer. He found one in the Russian Navy and received an admiral's commission from Catherine the Great herself. After participating in several battles in the Black Sea against the Turkish fleet, Ad-

miral Jones left Russia and retired to Paris. There he died in 1792 and was buried in a small Protestant cemetery. He was not put to final rest in the United States Naval Academy chapel until 1905, following an intensive search for his long-forgotten grave. ◆◆◆

"England Expects That Every Man Will Do His Duty!"

◆◆◆ *A quarter of a century later, twenty-eight miles south-east of Cádiz, Spain, less than sixteen miles west of Cape Trafalgar and just seaward of Gibraltar, a naval battle was fought that altered European patterns of conquest and weighted the balance scales of international sea power seemingly forever.*

On that fateful October Sunday in 1805, twenty-seven of the Royal Navy's "ships of the line" clashed with thirty-three similar vessels of the combined French and Spanish fleets. When evening came, Horatio Lord Nelson, Britain's already famous admiral, was dead at forty-seven years of age, and the enemy was virtually annihilated: sunk, captured, or fleeing in tatters back to ports of refuge.

To Napoleon the news was like a thunderclap. Waiting at that moment were 160,000 picked troops, commanded by his ablest marshal, poised to invade England. Now, without a fleet, how in the world could he launch his legions across even so narrow a body of water as the English Channel?

He could not.

His enemies, now regrouped and more leisurely, planned toward Bonaparte's Waterloo—ten years distant.

The daring, handsome Viscount Nelson had become Baron Nelson of the Nile after he had destroyed one French fleet at Aboukir Bay in the autumn of 1798. In previous engagements he had lost his right eye and right arm.

He capped earlier triumphs by eliminating the Danish fleet at the Battle of Copenhagen in 1801, which came to its climax on Good Friday. The confrontation grew out of a so-called armed neutrality, in which Russia, Prussia, Sweden, and Denmark—goaded on by the vindictive French —protested Great Britain's assumed right of search on the high seas.

The subsequent Peace of Amiens afforded Great Britain a respite for two years—time, also, for Lord Nelson to resume his attentions to Emma, the beautiful young wife of Sir William Hamilton, whom Nelson had first met when elderly Sir William was minister at the Court of Naples. Nelson fathered Emma's daughter, Horatia, so named in testament to his own vanity.

In 1803, Britain and France were back in death grips. Nelson returned to sea aboard the magnificent three-decked Victory, *mounting one hundred guns and carrying a crew of more than eight hundred officers and men. His flagship's length overall, slightly in excess of 227 feet, was comparable to the medium-sized coastal freighters and tankers of today.*

She was dwarfed, however, by the opposing Spanish flagship, the four-decked Santissima Trinidad, *carrying one hundred and thirty guns, said to be the world's largest man-*

of-war. The commander of the allied force, Vice Admiral Pierre de Villeneuve, unfurled his flag above the smaller French eighty-gun Bucentaure. *Six years Nelson's junior, Villeneuve was overcautious and dissatisfied with his captains.*

Nelson "in a fever," as he professed, to find Villeneuve, combed the shores of the Mediterranean from Gibraltar to Alexandria and then sailed across the Atlantic to the West Indies and back without finding a trace of his foe. Finally the Admiralty was informed by one of its ship commanders that Villeneuve's fleet was at Cádiz.

The Battle of Trafalgar took place on October 21, 1805. Sir William Beatty, "Physician Extraordinary to His Majesty of Scotland," was surgeon of the Victory, *and his account of the battle, despite its "dated" style, remains the most graphic extant.*

Dr. Beatty recounted how Nelson sailed toward his opponents through shoaly waters in light, uncertain winds. As the Admiral did so, he hoisted the flag message, "England expects that every man will do his duty!"

At first, Lord Nelson had dictated the curious phraseology, "England confides . . . but the signals officer suggested that "expects" be substituted since there was a code signal for "expect." "Confide" would have had to be tediously spelled out letter by letter. Either verb was part of a theatric gesture that evoked from Vice Admiral Cuthbert Collingwood, second in command, the comment, "We all know what we have to do!"

The engagement commenced with the enemy's taking

aim on the Royal Sovereign, *Collingwood's flagship. Dr. Beatty then recounted:* ◆◆◆

The enemy began to fire on the *Royal Sovereign* at thirty minutes past eleven o'clock; in ten minutes after which she placed herself under the stern of the *Santa Anna,* and commenced a fire on her. Lieutenant [John] Pasco, signal officer of the *Victory* [later a rear admiral] was heard to say while looking through his glass, "There is a topgallant-yard gone."

His Lordship eagerly asked, "Whose topgallant-yard is that gone? Is it the *Royal Sovereign*'s?" and on being answered by Lieutenant Pasco in the negative, and that it was the enemy's, he smiled and said: "Collingwood is doing well."

At 11:50 A.M., the enemy opened their fire on the Commander-in-Chief. They showed great coolness in the commencement of the battle; for as the *Victory* approached their line, their ships lying immediately ahead of her and across her bows fired only one gun at a time, to ascertain whether she was yet within their range. This was frequently repeated by eight or nine of their ships, till at length a shot passed through the *Victory*'s main-topgallant-sail; the hole in which being perceived by the enemy, they immediately opened their broadsides, supporting an awful and tremendous fire. In a very short time afterwards, Mr. John Scott, public secretary to the Commander-in-Chief, was killed by a cannon-shot while in conversation with Captain [Thomas M.] Hardy [commanding the *Victory*].

Lord Nelson being then near them, Captain Adair of the Marines, with the assistance of a seaman, endeavoured to remove the body from His Lordship's sight: but he had already observed the fall of his secretary; and now said with anxiety, "Is that poor Scott that is gone?" and on being answered in the affirmative by Captain Adair he replied, "Poor fellow!"

Lord Nelson and Captain Hardy walked the quarterdeck in conversation for some time after this, while the enemy kept up an incessant raking fire. A double-headed shot struck one of the parties of Marines drawn up on the poop, and killed eight of them; His Lordship, perceiving this, ordered Captain Adair to disperse his men round the ship, that they might not suffer so much from being together.

In a few minutes afterwards a shot struck the forebrace-bits on the quarterdeck, and passed between Lord Nelson and Captain Hardy; a splinter from the bits bruising Captain Hardy's foot, and tearing the buckle from his shoe.

They both instantly stopped; and were observed by the officers on deck to survey each other with inquiring looks, each supposing the other to be wounded. His Lordship then smiled, and said: "This is too warm work, Hardy, to last long"; and declared that "through all the battles he had been in, he had never witnessed more cool courage than was displayed by the *Victory*'s crew on this occasion."

The *Victory* by this time, having approached close to the enemy's van, had suffered very severely without firing a single gun, excepting one accidentally discharged whilst going down to the enemy: she had lost about twenty men killed, and had about thirty wounded. Her mizzen-topmast, and all her studding-sails and their booms, on both sides were shot away; the enemy's fire being chiefly directed at her rigging, with a view to disable her before she could close with them.

The enemy's fire continued to be pointed so high throughout the engagement that the *Victory* did not lose a man on her lower deck, had only two wounded on that deck, and these by musket balls.

At 12:04 P.M. she opened her fire, from both sides of her decks, upon the enemy; when Captain Hardy represented to His Lordship that "it appeared impracticable to pass through the enemy's line without going on board some one of their ships." Lord Nelson answered, "I cannot help it: it does not signify which we run on board of; go on board which you please; take your choice."

At 12:20 the tiller-ropes being shot away, Mr. Atkinson, the master, was ordered below to get the helm put to port; which being done, the *Victory* was soon run on board the *Redoutable* [a French ship] of seventy-four guns. On coming alongside and nearly on board of her, that ship fired her broadside into the *Victory,* and immediately let down her lower-deck ports; which, as has been since learnt, was done to prevent her from being boarded through them by the *Victory*'s crew. She never fired a great gun after this single broadside.

A few minutes after this, the *Temeraire* [a British ship] fell likewise on board of the *Redoutable,* on the side opposite to the *Victory;* having also an enemy's ship, said to be *La Fougueux* [French] on board of *her* on her other side:

so that the extraordinary and unprecedented circumstance occurred here, of *four* ships of the line being *on board of each other* in the heat of battle; forming as compact a tier as if they had been moored together, their heads lying all the same way.

The *Temeraire,* as was just before mentioned, was between the *Redoutable* and *La Fougueux.*

The *Redoutable* commenced a heavy fire of musketry from the tops, which was continued for a considerable time with destructive effect to the *Victory*'s crew; her great guns however being silent, it was supposed at different times that she had surrendered; and in consequence of this opinion, the *Victory* twice ceased firing upon her, by orders transmitted from the quarterdeck.

At this period, scarcely a person in the *Victory* escaped unhurt who was exposed on the upper deck to the enemy's musketry: but there were frequent huzzas and cheers heard from between the decks, in token of the surrender of different of the enemy's ships. An incessant fire was kept up from both sides of the *Victory:* her starboard guns played upon the *Santissima Trinidad* and the *Bucentaure;* and the starboard guns of the middle and lower decks were depressed, and fired with a diminished charge of powder, and three shot each, into the *Redoutable.* This mode of firing was adopted by Lieutenants Williams, King, Yule, and Brown, to obviate the danger of the *Temeraire*'s suffering from the *Victory*'s shot passing through the *Redoutable;* which must have been the case if the usual quantity of powder, and the common elevation, had been given to the guns. A circumstance occurred in this situation, which showed in a most striking manner the cool intrepidity of the officers and men stationed on the lower deck of the *Victory.*

When the guns on this deck were run out, their muzzles came into contact with the *Redoutable*'s side; and consequently at every discharge there was reason to fear that the enemy would take fire, and both the *Victory* and the *Temeraire* be involved in her flames. Here then was seen the astonishing spectacle of the fireman of each gun standing ready with a bucketful of water, which as soon as his gun was discharged he dashed into the enemy through the holes made in her side by the shot.

It was from this ship, the *Redoutable,* that Lord Nelson received his mortal wound. About fifteen minutes past one o'clock, which was in the heat of the engagement, he was walking the middle of the quarterdeck with Captain Hardy, and in the act of turning near the hatchway with his face toward the poop of the *Victory,* when the fatal ball was fired from the enemy's mizzen-top by a rifle or musket marksman high up on an aftermast; which, from the situation of the two ships then on board of each other, was brought just abaft, and rather below, the *Victory*'s main-yard, and of course not more than fifteen yards distant from that part of the deck where His Lordship stood. The ball struck the epaulette on his left shoulder and penetrated his chest.

He fell with his face on the deck. Captain Hardy, who was on his right (the side furthest from the *Redoutable*) and advanced some steps before His Lordship, on turning round, saw the Sergeant Major (Secker) of Marines with two seamen raising him from the deck; where he had fallen on the same spot on which his secretary had been killed a little before, with whose blood His Lordship's clothes were much stained. Captain Hardy expressed a hope that he was not severely wounded; to which the gallant Chief replied: "They have done for me at last, Hardy."

"I hope not," answered Captain Hardy.

"Yes," replied His Lordship; "my backbone is shot through."

Captain Hardy desired the seamen to convey His Lordship to the cockpit; and now two incidents occurred strikingly characteristic of this great man, and strongly marking that energy and reflection which in his heroic mind rose superior even to the immediate consideration of his own awful condition. While the men were carrying him down the ladder from the middle deck, His Lordship remarked that the tiller-ropes were not yet replaced; and desired one of the midshipmen stationed there to go upon the quarterdeck and remind Captain Hardy of that circumstance, and request that new ones should be immediately rove. Having thus expressed himself, he took his handkerchief from his pocket and covered his face with it, that he might be conveyed to the cockpit at this crisis unnoticed by the crew.

Several wounded officers and about forty men were likewise carried to the surgeon for assistance just at this time; and some others had breathed their last during their conveyance below. The surgeon had just examined two officers, and found that they were dead when his attention was arrested by several of the wounded calling to him, "Mr. Beatty, Lord Nelson is here: Mr. Beatty, the Admiral is wounded."

The surgeon now, on looking round, saw the handkerchief fall from His Lordship's face; when the stars on his coat, which also had been covered by it, appeared. Mr. Burke, the purser, and the surgeon ran immediately to the assistance of His Lordship, and took him from the arms of the seamen who had carried him below.

In conveying him to one of the midshipmen's berths, they stumbled, but recovered themselves without falling. Lord Nelson then inquired who were supporting him; and when the surgeon informed him, His Lordship replied, "Ah, Mr. Beatty! You can do nothing for me. I have but a short time to live: my back is shot through."

The surgeon said he hoped the wound was not so dangerous as His Lordship imagined, and that he might still survive long to enjoy his glorious victory. The Reverend Doctor Scott, who had been absent in another part of the cockpit administering lemonade to the wounded, now came instantly to His Lordship; and in the anguish of grief wrung his hands, and said: "Alas, Beatty, how prophetic you were!" alluding to the apprehensions expressed by the surgeon for His Lordship's safety previous to the battle.

His Lordship was laid upon a bed, stripped of his clothes, and covered with a sheet. While this was effecting, he said to Doctor Scott, "Doctor, I told you so. Doctor, I am gone"; and after a short pause he added in a low voice, "I have to leave Lady Hamilton, and my adopted daughter Horatia, as a legacy to my country."

The surgeon then examined the wound, assuring His Lordship that he would not put him to much pain in endeavouring to discover the course of the ball; which he soon found had penetrated deep into the chest, and had probably lodged in the spine. This being explained to His Lordship, he replied he was confident his back was shot through.

The back was then examined externally, but without any injury being perceived; on which His Lordship was requested by the surgeon to make him acquainted with all his sensations. He replied that he felt a gush of blood every minute within his breast: that he had no feeling in the lower part of his body: and that his breathing was difficult, and attended with very severe pain about that part of the spine where he was confident that the ball had struck; for, said he, "I felt it break my back."

These symptoms, but more particularly the gush of blood which His Lordship complained of, together with the state of his pulse, indicated to the surgeon the hopeless situation of the case; but till after the victory was ascertained and announced to His Lordship, the true nature of his wound was concealed by the surgeon from all on board except only Captain Hardy, Doctor Scott, Mr. Burke, and Messrs. Smith and Westemburg, the assistant surgeons.

The *Victory*'s crew cheered whenever they observed an enemy's ship surrender. On one of these occasions, Lord Nelson anxiously inquired what was the cause of it. . . . Lieutenant Pasco, who lay wounded at some distance from His Lordship, raised himself up and told him that another ship had struck.

Lord Nelson now desired Mr. Cuevalier, his steward, to turn him upon his right side; which being effected, His Lordship said, "I wish I had not left the deck, for I shall soon be gone."

He afterwards became very low; his breathing was oppressed and his voice faint. He said to Doctor Scott, "Doctor, I have not been a *great* sinner," and after a short pause, *"Remember,* that I leave Lady Hamilton and my daughter Horatia as a legacy to my country: and," added he, "never forget Horatia."

His thirst now increased; and he called for, "Drink, drink," "Fan, fan," and "Rub, rub"; addressing himself in the last case to Doctor Scott, who had been rubbing His Lordship's breast with his hand from which he found relief. These words he spoke in a very rapid manner, which rendered his articulation difficult; but he every now and then, with evident increase of pain, made a greater effort with his vocal powers, and pronounced distinctly these last words, "Thank God, I have done my duty," and this pious expression he continued to repeat as long as he was able to give it utterance.

His Lordship became speechless in about fifteen minutes after Captain Hardy left him. Doctor Scott and Mr. Burke, who had all along sustained the bed under his shoulders (which raised him in nearly a semi-recumbent posture, the only one that was supportable to him), forbore to disturb him by speaking to him; and when he had remained speechless about five minutes, His Lordship's steward went to the surgeon, who had been a short time occupied with the wounded in another part of the cockpit, and stated his apprehensions that His Lordship was dying.

The surgeon immediately repaired to him, and found him on the verge of dissolution. He knelt down by his side, and took up his hand; which was cold, and the pulse gone from the wrist.

On the surgeon's laying his hand on his forehead, which was likewise cold, His Lordship opened his eyes, looked up, and shut them again. The surgeon again left him, and returned to the wounded who required his assistance; but was not absent five minutes before the steward announced to him that he believed His Lordship had "expired."

The surgeon returned, and found that the report was but too well founded: His Lordship had breathed his last, at thirty minutes past four o'clock: at which momentous period Doctor Scott was in the act of rubbing His Lordship's breast and Mr. Burke supporting the bed under his shoulders, which offices they had been engaged in for a considerable time . . .

(Immediately after His Lordship expired, Captain Hardy went on board the *Royal Sovereign,* to communicate the melancholy event, and the nature of His Lordship's last orders, to Admiral Collingwood.)

From the time of His Lordship's being wounded till his death, a period of about two hours and forty-five minutes elapsed; but a knowledge of the decisive victory which was gained, he acquired of Captain Hardy within the first hour-and-a-quarter of this period. A partial cannonade, however, was still maintained, in consequence of the enemy's running ships passing the British at different points; and the last distant guns which were fired at their van ships that were making off, were heard a minute or two before His Lordship expired.

A steady and continued fire was kept up by the *Victory*'s starboard guns on the *Redoubtable,* for about fifteen minutes after Lord Nelson was wounded; in which short period Captain Adair and about eighteen seamen and Marines were killed, and Lieutenant Bligh, Mr. Palmer, midshipman, and twenty seamen and Marines, wounded, by the enemy's musketry alone. The *Redoutable* had been on fire twice, in her forechains and on her forecastle: she had likewise succeeded in throwing a few hand grenades into the *Victory,* which set fire to some ropes and canvas on the booms.

The cry of "Fire!" was now circulated throughout the ship, and even reached the cockpit, without producing the degree of sensation which might be expected on such an awful occasion: the crew soon extinguished the fire on the booms, and then immediately turned their attention to that on board the enemy; which they likewise put out by throwing buckets of water from the gangway into the enemy's chains and forecastle, thus furnishing another admirable instance of deliberate intrepidity.

At 1:30 P.M. the *Redoutable*'s musketry having ceased, and her colors being struck, the *Victory*'s men endeavoured to get on board her: but this was found impracticable; for, though the two ships were still in contact, yet the topsides or upper-works of both fell in so much on their upper decks, that there was a great space (perhaps fourteen feet or more) between their gangways; and the enemy's ports being down, she could not be boarded from the *Victory*'s lower or middle deck. Several seamen volunteered their services to Lieutenant Quilliam, to jump overboard, swim under the *Redoutable*'s bows, and endeavor to get up there; but Captain Hardy refused to permit this. The prize, however, and the *Victory,* fell off from each other; and their separation was believed to be the effect of the concussion produced by the *Victory*'s fire, assisted by the helm of the latter being put to starboard.

Messrs. Ogilvie and Collingwood, midshipmen of the *Victory*, were sent in a small boat to take charge of the prize, which they effected. The two had just boarded the *Redoutable*, and got their men out of the boat, when a shot from the enemy's van ships that were making off cut the boat adrift. About ten minutes after taking possession of her, a midshipman came to her from the *Temeraire*; and had hardly ascended the poop, when a shot from one of those ships took off his leg. The French officers, seeing the firing continued on the prize by their own countrymen, entreated the English midshipmen to quit the deck, and accompany them below. The unfortunate midshipman of the *Temeraire* was carried to the French surgeon, who was ordered to give his immediate attendance to him in preference to his own wounded; his leg was amputated, but he died the same night. The *Redoutable* suffered so much from shot received between wind and water, that she sunk while in tow of the *Swiftsure* on the following evening, when the gale came on; and out of a crew originally consisting of more than eight hundred men, about a hundred and thirty only were saved, but she had lost above three hundred from the battle.

About twenty of the *Redoutable*'s guns were dismounted in the action. Those on that side of her lower deck opposed to the *Victory*, were all dismounted except five or six.

It is by no means certain, though highly probable, that Lord Nelson was particularly aimed at by the enemy. There were only two Frenchmen left alive in the mizzen top of the

Redoutable at the time of His Lordship's being wounded, and by the hands of one of these he fell.

—*Authentic Narrative of the Death of Lord Nelson,*
by William Beatty, M.D., W. Mason, London, 1825

◆◆◆ *The losses at Trafalgar were fantastic by the measure of any era of naval warfare, including the present. The British sustained 2,500 casualties, the enemy 7,000, with a high proportion of those killed or drowned. The entire complements of the* Berwick *and* Fougueux, *for example, were with those French warships when they foundered in the next day's gale. Rescue parties were somewhat luckier in saving some of the crew from the towering* Santissima Trinidad, *including the ship's cat, before "the waves passed over her, she gave a lurch and went down," as one awestruck British tar observed.*

Admiral Villeneuve, taken prisoner, might as well have perished with his ships. Although shortly released by the British, for whose treatment of him he expressed only praise, he could not rid himself of a feeling of guilt for losing an entire fleet. He committed suicide the next year.

Lord Nelson's remains, embalmed by Dr. Beatty in a cask of brandy, were not returned to London until 1806. More than 30,000 mourners lined the Thames Embankment on January 9 in final tribute to "the first of the moderns" among naval leaders, as he would be described by Joseph Conrad. He was laid to rest in a crypt of St. Paul's Cathedral, beside the Empire's immortals in the many fields of human endeavor and accomplishment. ◆◆◆

Thunder Off Cherbourg

◆◆◆ *Half a century after Trafalgar, the arena of naval warfare was still as broad as the British and their enemies had always found it. But the contestants had changed. Now, it was North against the South in America's bloody, tragic Civil War, also labeled War of the Rebellion and the War of Secession.*

Federal gunboats scoured the seven seas in search of Rebel raiders, one of the most celebrated of which was C.S.S. Alabama. *This English-built Confederate cruiser was to have a date with destiny one bright Sunday morning, June 19, 1864, off the port of Cherbourg, France, in a confrontation with the powerful Federal screw sloop* Kearsarge. *In two years the* Alabama *had burned fifty-two merchant vessels, captured and ransomed ten, and sold one. More than two hundred neutrals had been examined and allowed to proceed.*

Her captain was Maryland-born Raphael Semmes, then fifty-six, whose long career had included duty in the old Constellation *and the blockading of Vera Cruz during the*

Mexican War. He resigned his commission in the United States Navy two months before Sumter was fired upon (April 12, 1861) and took command of the Sumter, *named after Fort Sumter, in Charleston Harbor, the fall of which on April 14, 1861, signaled the start of the Civil War. This vessel preyed on Union merchantmen for two years.*

Semmes, a dour, fanatical sort with sad, smoldering eyes and a waxed mustache, hated the North. "Devoid of Christian charity" and "hyenas" were among the epithets hurled by this singularly humorless man toward his erst-while countrymen. With a lack of objectivity for a profes-sional officer, contrasting with men such as Lee or Stonewall Jackson, Semmes pursued his raider's work with vengeful-ness.

His opponent, Captain John A. Winslow, of the Kear-sarge, *was a former shipmate. Two years younger and a Carolinian, he tended to heaviness, was blind in one eye, and was not as prepossessing physically as the slender, ascetic Semmes. Winslow, however, was loyal to "Old Glory."*

Winslow's command, at 1,000 tons, was almost the same size as the Alabama. *Both ships, with sail, could make fifteen knots and required crews of one hundred and fifty officers and men. The* Kearsarge's *main advantage lay in her two 11-inch pivot guns, rather than in numbers of naval rifles, contrasted with the* Alabama's *largest gun: 8-inch. She also carried one-and-one-half-inch-thick chain armor over her sides, a fact which was to inspire the bitter observation from Semmes: "The days of chivalry are past."*

On June 11, 1864, the Alabama *dropped anchor in the splendid harbor of Cherbourg, with its picturesque terra-*

cotta roofs of the many quayside structures. The ship badly needed hull and engine work, the crew—largely British—rest and also fresh clothing.

Two days later, Semmes reported to Samuel Barron, a flag officer of the Confederate Navy in Paris: ◆◆◆

Sir: I have just been informed by the Hon. Mr. John Slidell [Confederate emissary to France] of your presence in Paris. I have the honor to report to you the arrival of this ship at this place in want of repairs. She will require to be recoppered, refastened in some places, and to have her boilers pretty extensively repaired, all of which will probably detain her a couple of months. I shall have sufficient funds at my command to pay off officers and crew, but will require money for repairs. As soon as I receive permission from the admiral here to go into dock, I propose to give my men leave for an extended run on shore, many of them being in indifferent health, in consequence of their long detention on shipboard and on salt diet. The officers also will expect a similar indulgence.

As for myself, my health has suffered so much from a constant and harassing service of three years, almost continuously at sea, that I shall have to ask for relief.

The Kearsarge, *sniffing the* Alabama's *scent for many months, hove to on the fourteenth outside the breakwater. A routine check with the American consul revealed that at last the quarry was at bay.*

Semmes, who had put ashore prisoners taken from the

merchant ships he had sunk, at once interpreted the Kear-*sarge's* presence as the challenge for a duel. Like a gentle-*man* who fancies his honor is on the scales, the Confederate *captain* hastened a note to his old comrade, Winslow:

"I desire you to say to the United States consul that my intention is to fight the Kearsarge *as soon as I can make the* necessary arrangements. . . . I beg she will not depart be-*fore I am ready to go out.*"

In his own diary, Semmes noted with unwarranted opti-*mism,* "The two ships are so equally matched . . ."

The next day, the fifteenth, the French Minister of Ma-*rine,* though sanctioning coaling, advised the Confederate *man-of-war* through the Maritime Prefect at Cherbourg that *she could not be refitted:*

We cannot permit the *Alabama* to enter into one of our basins of the arsenal, that not being indispensable to place it in a state to go again to sea. This vessel can address itself to commerce (commercial accommodations) for urgent re-pairs which it has need of to enable it to go out, but the principles of neutrality recalled in my circular of the fifth of February do not permit us to give to one of the belligerents the means to augment its forces, and in some sort to rebuild itself; in fine it is not proper that one of the belligerents take without ceasing our ports, and especially our arsenals, as a base of their operations, and, so to say, as one of their own proper ports.

You will observe to the captain of the *Alabama* that he has not been forced to enter into Cherbourg by any accidents of the sea, and that he could altogether as well have touched at ports of Spain, of Portugal, of England, of Belgium, and of Holland.

As to the prisoners made by the *Alabama,* and who have been placed ashore, they are free from the time they have touched our soil. But they ought not to be delivered up to the *Kearsarge,* which is a Federal ship of war. This would be for the *Kearsarge* an augmentation of military force, and we can no more permit this for one of the belligerents than for the other."

On the sixteenth, William L. Dayton, United States Minister to France, wrote to Captain Winslow:

Sir: This will be delivered to you by my son and assistant secretary of legation. I have had a conversation this afternoon with Dr. Drouyn de Lhuys, minister of foreign affairs. He says they have given the *Alabama* notice that she must leave Cherbourg, but in the meantime you have come in and are watching the *Alabama,* and that this vessel is anxious to meet you, and he supposes you will attack her as soon as she gets three miles off the coast; that this will produce a fight which will be at best a fight in waters which may or may not be French waters, as accident may determine; that it would be offensive to the dignity of France to have a fight under such circumstances, and France will not permit it; that the *Alabama* shall not attack you, nor you her, within the three miles, nor on or about that distance off.

Under such circumstances I do not suppose that they would have, on principles of international law, the least right to interfere with you if three miles off the coast, but if you lose nothing by fighting six or seven miles off the coast instead of three you had best do so. You know better than I (who have little or no knowledge of the relative strength of the two vessels) whether the pretense of the *Alabama* of a readiness to meet you is more than a pretense, and I do not wish you to sacrifice any advantage if you have it. I suggest only that you avoid all unnecessary trouble with France, but if the *Alabama* can be taken without violating any rules of international law, and may be lost if such a principle is yielded, you know what the Government would expect of you. You will of course yield no real advantage to which you are entitled, while you are careful to so act as to make uselessly no unnecessary complications with this Government. I ought to add that Mr. Seward's dispatch, dated 20th May, 1864, was in the following words:

"The *Niagara* will proceed with as much dispatch as possible to cruise in European waters, and the *Dictator,* so soon as she shall be ready for sea (which is expected to be quite soon), will follow her, unless in the meantime advices from yourself and Mr. Adams shall be deemed to furnish reasons for a change of purpose in that prospect."

That you may understand exactly the condition of things here in regard to the *Alabama,* I send you herewith a copy of a communication from the minister of marine to the naval prefect at Cherbourg, furnished me by the minister of foreign affairs.

Then, on the seventeenth, Dayton wrote to Secretary of State William H. Seward in Washington:

You will doubtless have received before this notice of the arrival of the *Alabama* in the port of Cherbourg, and my protest to this Government against the extension of any accommodations to this vessel. Mr. Drouyn de Lhuys yesterday informed me that they had made up their minds to this course, and he gave me a copy of the written directions given by the minister of marine to the vice admiral, maritime prefect at Cherbourg, a translation of which accompanies this dispatch. But he, at the same time, informed me that the United States ship of war the *Kearsarge* had appeared off the port of Cherbourg, and there was danger of an immediate fight between those vessels; that the *Alabama* professed its entire readiness to meet the *Kearsarge,* and he believed that each would attack the other as soon as they were three miles off the coast; that a sea fight would thus be got up in the face of France, and at a distance from their coast within reach of the guns used on shipboard in these days; that the distance to which the neutral right of an adjoining government extended itself from the coast was unsettled, and that the reason for the old rule, which assumed that three miles was the outermost reach of a cannon shot, no longer existed, and that, in a word, a fight on or about such a distance from their coast would be offensive to the dignity of France, and they would not permit it.

I told him that no other rule than the three-mile rule was known or recognized as a principle of international law, but if a fight were to take place, and we would lose nothing and risk nothing by its being further off, I had of course no objection. I had no wish to wound the susceptibilities of France by getting up a fight within a distance which makes the cannon shot liable to fall on the coast.

I asked him if he would put his views and wishes on the question in writing, and he promised me to do so. I wrote to Captain Winslow this morning, and herewith enclose you a copy of my letter. I have carefully avoided in this communication anything which would tend to make the *Kearsarge* risk anything by yielding what seemed to me to be an admitted right.

To deliver this letter and understand some other matters in respect to the alleged sale of the two clipper ships at Bordeaux, I have sent my son to Cherbourg.

Early on June 19, following divine services on deck, the quartermaster of the Kearsarge *logged:*

Lying off and on off Cherbourg. Moderate breeze from the westward; weather, b.c. [blue sky, cloud]. At 10:20 A.M. discovered the *Alabama* steaming out of the port of Cherbourg, accompanied by a French ironclad steamer and a fore-and-aft rigged steamer, showing the white English ensign and a yacht flag. Beat to general quarters and cleared for action. Steamed ahead, standing offshore, being distant from the land about two leagues; altered our course and approached the *Alabama*.

Winslow, in his report to Secretary of the Navy Gideon Welles, continued:

. . . The day being fine, with a hazy atmosphere, wind moderate from the westward, with little sea, the position of the *Kearsarge* at ten o'clock was near the buoy which marks the line of shoals to the eastward of Cherbourg, and distant about three miles from the eastern entrance, which bore to the southward and westward. At 10:20 o'clock the *Alabama* was descried coming out of the western entrance, accompanied by the *Couroone* (ironclad).

I had, in an interview with the admiral at Cherbourg, assured him that in the event of an action occurring with the *Alabama* the position of the ships should be so far offshore that the question could not be advanced about the line of jurisdiction. Accordingly, to perfect this object, and with the double purpose of drawing the *Alabama* so far offshore that if disabled she could not return, directed the ship's head seaward, and cleared for action with the battery pivoted to starboard.

Having attained a point about seven miles from the shore, the head of the *Kearsarge* was turned short round and the ship steered directly for the *Alabama,* my purpose being to run her down, or, if circumstances did not warrant it, to close in with her. Hardly had the *Kearsarge* come round before the *Alabama* sheered, presented her starboard battery, and slowed her engines.

On approaching her at long range of about a mile, she opened her full broadside, the shot cutting some of our rigging and going over and alongside of us. Immediately I ordered more speed, but in two minutes the *Alabama* had loaded and again fired another broadside, and following it with a third, without damaging us except in rigging.

Semmes reported on the same time period to Samuel Barron, a Confederate officer of flag rank, in Paris, as follows:

I steamed out of the harbor of Cherbourg between nine and ten o'clock on the morning of June 19 for the purpose of engaging the enemy's steamer *Kearsarge*, which had been lying off and on the port for several days previously. After clearing the harbor we descried the enemy, with his head offshore, at a distance of about nine miles. We were three-quarters of an hour in coming up with him.

I had previously pivoted my guns to starboard, and made all my preparations for engaging the enemy on that side. When within about a mile and a quarter of the enemy he suddenly wheeled, and bringing his head inshore presented his starboard battery to me. By this time we were distant about one mile from each other, when I opened on him with solid shot, to which he replied in a few minutes, and the engagement became active on both sides.

Winslow continued:

We had now arrived within about 900 yards of her, and I was apprehensive that another broadside, nearly raking as it was, would prove disastrous. Accordingly, I ordered the *Kearsarge* sheered, and opened on the *Alabama*.

The position of the vessels was now broadside and broadside, but it was soon apparent that Captain Semmes did not seek close action. I became then fearful, lest after some fighting he would again make for the shore. To defeat this, I determined to keep full speed on, and with a port helm to run under the stern of the *Alabama* and rake, if he did not prevent it by sheering and keeping his broadside to us. He adopted this mode as a preventive, and as a consequence the *Alabama* was forced with a full head of steam into a circular track during the engagement.

The effect of this maneuver was such that at the last of the action, when the *Alabama* would have made off, she was near five miles from the shore and had the action continued from the first in parallel lines, with her head inshore, the line of jurisdiction would no doubt have been reached. The firing of the *Alabama* from the first was rapid and wild. Toward the close of the action her firing became better.

Our men, who had been cautioned against rapid firing without direct aim, were much more deliberate, and the instructions given to point the heavy guns below rather than above the water line and clear the deck with the lighter ones was fully observed. I had endeavored with a port helm to close in with the *Alabama,* but it was not until just before the close of the action that we were in position to use grape.

The effect of the training of our men was evident. Nearly every shot from our guns was telling fearfully on the *Alabama,* and on the seventh rotation on the circular track she winded, setting fore-trysail and two jibs, with head inshore.

The enemy now pressed his ship under a full head of steam, and to prevent our passing each other too speedily, and to keep our respective broadsides bearing it became necessary to fight in a circle, the two ships steaming around a common center and preserving a distance from each other of from a quarter to half a mile.

Semmes:

The enemy was much damaged but to what extent it is now impossible to tell. It is believed he was badly crippled.

My officers and men behaved steadily and gallantly. Where all behaved so well it would be invidious to particularize; but I cannot deny myself the pleasure of saying that Mr. [John McIntosh] Kell, my first lieutenant, deserves great credit for the fine condition in which the ship went into action, with regard to her battery, magazine and shell rooms; also that he rendered me great assistance by his coolness and judgment as the fight proceeded. The enemy was heavier than myself, both in ship, battery, and crew; but I did not know until the action was over that she was also ironclad.

The enemy's shot and shell soon began to tell upon our hull, knocking down, killing, and disabling a number of men in different parts of the ship.

Perceiving that our shell, though apparently exploding against the enemy's sides, was doing but little damage, I returned to solid firing, and from this time onward alternated with shot and shell. After the lapse of about one hour and ten minutes our ship was ascertained to be in a sinking condition, the enemy's shell having exploded in the sides and between decks, opening large apertures, through which the water rushed with great rapidity.

For some few minutes I had hopes of being able to reach the French coast, for which purpose I gave our ship all steam and set such of the fore-and-aft sails as were available. The ship filled so rapidly, however, that before we had made much progress the fires were extinguished in the furnaces, and we were evidently on the point of sinking.

Naval Surgeon John Browne, aboard the Kearsarge, *added something to what was happening below decks:*

The action continued for eighteen minutes without casualties. Then a 68-pound Blakely shell passed through the starboard bulwarks below main rigging, exploded upon the quarterdeck, and wounded three of the crew of the pivot gun. One, William Gowin, ordinary seaman, received a compound fracture of left femur at lower and middle third, and tibia and fibula, upper third, complicating the knee joint.

Winslow:

Her speed was now retarded, and, by winding, her port broadside was presented to us with only two guns bearing, not having been able, as I learned afterwards, to shift over but one.

I saw now that she was at our mercy, and a few more guns, well directed, brought down her flag. I was unable to ascertain whether they had been hauled down or shot away, but a white flag having been displayed over the stern, our fire was reserved.

Two minutes had not more than elapsed before she again opened on us with the two guns on the port side. This drew our fire again, and the *Kearsarge* was immediately steamed ahead, and laid across her bows for raking. The white flag was still flying, and our fire was again reserved.

Semmes:

I now hauled down my colors to prevent the further destruction of life, and dispatched a boat to inform the enemy of our condition. Although we were now but 400 yards from each other, the enemy fired upon me five times after my colors had been struck, dangerously wounding several of my men. It is charitable to suppose that a ship of war of a Christian nation could not have done this intentionally. We now turned all our exertions toward the wounded and such of the boys as were unable to swim. These were dispatched in my quarter boats, the only boats remaining to me, the waist boat having been torn to pieces.

Some twenty minutes after my furnace fires had been extinguished and the ship being on the point of settling, every man, in obedience to a previous order which had been given to the crew, jumped overboard and endeavored to save himself. There was no appearance of any boat coming to me from the enemy until after the ship went down.

Fortunately, however, the steam yacht *Deerhound*, owned by a gentlemen of Lancashire, England [Mr. John Lancaster], who was himself on board steamed up in the midst of my drowning men and rescued a number of both officers and men from the water.

I was fortunate enough myself thus to escape to the shelter of the neutral flag, together with about forty others, all told. About this time the *Kearsarge* sent one, then, tardily, another boat.

Winslow:

Shortly after this her boats were seen to be lowering, and an officer in one of them came alongside and informed us that the ship had surrendered and was fast sinking. In twenty minutes from this time, the *Alabama* went down, her mainmast, which had been shot, breaking near the head as she sank, and her bow rising high out of the water as her stern rapidly settled.

Naval Surgeon John Browne, aboard the Kearsarge, *wrote as a curious postscript:*

This Sunday's naval duel was fought in the presence of more than 15,000 spectators who, upon the heights of Cherbourg, the breakwater, and rigging of men-of-war, witnessed "the last of the *Alabama*." Among them were the captains, their families, and crews of two merchant ships burnt by the daring cruiser a few days before her arrival at Cherbourg, where they were landed in a nearly destitute condition.

Many spectators were provided with spyglasses and campstools. The *Kearsarge* was burning Newcastle coals, and the *Alabama* Welsh coals, the difference in the amount of smoke enabling the movements of each ship to be distinctly traced. An excursion train from Paris arrived in the morning, bringing hundreds of pleasure seekers, who were unexpectedly favored with the spectacle of a sea fight. A French gentleman at Boulogne-sur-Mer assured me that the fight was the conversation of Paris for more than a week.

Our total loss in killed and wounded is thirty, to wit, nine killed and twenty-one wounded [compared with the one death and two injuries on the *Kearsarge*].

> —*Official Records of the Union and Confederate Navies in the War of the Rebellion*
> (Series 1, No. 3), Government Printing House, Washington, 1896

◆◆◆ *Semmes was one of 115 officers and men who reached sanctuary either in England or France. This left barely 51 prisoners aboard the* Kearsarge, *most of whom were paroled, much to Secretary Welles' annoyance. In fact, on behalf of the Navy, he disavowed the parole.*

The Alabama *had sunk about five miles northeast of the Cherbourg breakwater in approximately 270 feet of water. No attempts, so far as is known, have ever been made by divers to inspect the famous wreck in the English Channel.*

The Confederate captain made his way to the Secessionist States. He commanded three ironclads and five gunboats in the James River at the fall of Richmond. He spent his postwar years teaching, lecturing, practicing law, and writing his memoirs. Somewhat mellower with his accumulating years, Semmes would recall nostalgically, "We fought her until she no longer could swim—then we gave her to the waves."

He died in 1877 near his home in Mobile, Alabama.

After this famous naval action, Winslow became a popular hero in the North. He was promoted to Commodore and from 1870 to 1872, as a rear admiral, commanded the Pacific Squadron. By then, in failing health, Winslow sought to regain his strength by a voyage to South America and long recuperation there. He died, however, at Boston in 1873, where he is buried in Forest Hill Cemetery.

Final amen to the Alabama *saga had been pronounced the preceding year when an International Tribunal of Arbitration agreed that Great Britain owed the United States $15,500,000 damages for the depredations caused by Captain Semmes' cruiser and by two other English-built raiders, the* Florida *and* Shenandoah. ◆◆◆

"Four Bells! Captain Drayton, Go Ahead!"

♦♦♦ *The* Alabama *had been resting on the bottom of the English Channel but six weeks when another dramatic engagement ended with a Union victory. Rear Admiral David Glasgow Farragut dared the forts of Mobile Bay to dispute his entrance.*

The beautiful bay, sweeping thirty-five miles inland and seven to fifteen miles across, provided one of the most ample anchorages of the Gulf Coast. It was a coveted prize, even more so than the Alabama port city itself. Not surprisingly, the defenses were calculated to thwart any but the most determined assault.

The bay's bastions consisted of three forts. Morgan, the most glowering, mounted sixty guns, largely 10-inchers, within thick masonry walls. It was situated at the end of a wasplike sandpit, Mobile Point, on the eastern shore. Fort Gaines, straddling the approaches, on Dauphin Island, and Fort Powell on the northwestern side of the harbor, were relatively weak, although they augmented Morgan's batteries by thirty-four heavy cannon.

The Confederacy pinned its hopes upon the 209-foot ironclad ram Tennessee, *which was equipped with an underwater metal prow or "beak." She was escorted by three small, rather inconsequential gunboats.* Tennessee *carried the flag of Admiral Franklin Buchanan, in charge of the naval defenses of Mobile. He was the same officer who commanded the* Merrimac *during her historic duel with the U.S.S.* Monitor *at Hampton Roads, Virginia, when he had been seriously wounded.*

Buchanan asserted to the crew of the Tennessee, *"You shall not have it to say when you leave this vessel that you were not near enough to the enemy, for I will meet them . . . and if I fall, lay me on one side and go on with the fight!"*

Farragut had assembled a squadron of fourteen wooden steam frigates and four of the Monitor *class. The latter were iron-hulled vessels, with some thick wooden decking and side timbers as armor. These contrasted with conventional wooden-hulled craft with iron plates fastened on their sides —"ironclads." The sixty-four-year-old conqueror of New Orleans led in his magnificent flagship,* Hartford, *accompanied by a twin, the* Brooklyn. *Both were wooden men-of-war, relying entirely on their thick oak timbers for protection against shot and shell.*

While "Davy" Farragut, a sailor whose quick temper was well known, had protested the shortage of monitors and ironclads, he had also stated, in emotional outbursts, "Give me hearts of iron in ships of oak!"

Included in Farragut's fleet were two types of monitors. The Tecumseh *and* Manhattan *mounted single turrets, with two 15-inch guns.* Chickasaw *and* Winnebago *were double-turreted with four 11-inch guns. These revolving turrets were the sole targets presented to enemy gunners. A well-piloted monitor, therefore, was vulnerable only to mines.*

It was assumed that the remainder of the Northern fleet, whether blockading or on the offensive, would prevail through superiority of numbers. Even Hudson River ferry-boats had steamed to war, patrolling the mouths of southern rivers and estuaries.

In late July,1864, while General William T. Sherman was investing Atlanta, Farragut led more of his ships out of the naval base at Pensacola, Florida, toward Mobile, where the bulk of his fleet had been on blockade duty since the previous January. On August 4, he hove to in the main ship channel leading into the bay and waited for the powerful monitor Tecumseh. *Daringly, Farragut himself reconnoi-tered the approaches by steam launch. For several hours he remained in range of enemy guns.*

Satisfied that the forts could be passed the next dawn, the admiral lashed his ships together, two by two, like ani-mals going into the Ark. Their massed firepower far ex-ceeded that of the combined English, French, and Spanish fleets at Trafalgar.

What happened next is told in an historical society paper prepared after the war by William F. Hutchinson, of Rhode Island, an assistant surgeon aboard the frigate Lacka-wanna. ◆◆◆

One by one the more northern strongholds of the Rebel seacoast had fallen before the combined attacks of our gal-

lant army and navy, and at last all was in readiness to deal a
blow on the Gulf Coast which should blot out the most important station remaining in the possession of the Rebel
government. For three years, Mobile Bay, with its many
channels of entrance, its various and continually changing
bars, and its powerful defenses, had been a point whence
much successful blockade running had been carried on, and
wherein had been fitted out two of the boldest and most un-
scrupulous of the piratical rovers dignified by the name of
Confederate men-of-war.

Within its protecting forts lay the only remaining fleet of
the enemy, commanded by Admiral Buchanan in his flagship, the ram *Tennessee*. Between this officer and his ship
existed strong points of resemblance. He, the last and only
Confederate Admiral afloat—a stern, pitiless man, deaf to
all considerations save those of mistaken duty to a bad
cause, brave as a lion, and a superb officer: it—their stron-
gest, costliest and last ironclad, their boast and pride—they
were indeed fitted to go down together.

It had become necessary to break up this nest of treason,
for the blockade runners, barred from their whilom ports by
the victorious progress of our arms, came here in great
numbers, laden with vast quantities of munitions of war and
provisions; and, notwithstanding the most painstaking vigi-
lance on the part of the fleet, few dark nights and no single
stormy one passed without one or more of these "carrier
doves," as the Southern dames called them, finding their
way into the beleaguered harbor.

This reason determined Admiral Farragut to hasten the
attack which he had long held in contemplation, and a call

was made upon General Edward Canby for a military force sufficient to cooperate with the navy and hold the forts when captured. To this duty was assigned Major General Gordon Granger, with a sufficient force of artillery and infantry.

The morning of August 4, 1864, dawned beautifully clear, and the blue waters of the Mexican Gulf stretched away southward a thousand miles to the Venezuelan shore, while to the north its waves splashed lazily in a tropical sun against the white sand of Dauphin Island and Mobile Point, between which curved the winding channel of entrance to the bay. Twenty-six stately ships of war (including tenders and supply vessels) lay at anchor on the bar six miles from land, their long pennants and colors clinging to the spars, while from one to the other flashed small boats with their crews of bluejackets, and with gold-laced officers in the stern sheets, from whose uniforms the sunbeams glinted merrily. Instead of being away on their stations, deployed in such a manner as to draw a cordon of guard around the harbor entrance, the ships were massed around one central vessel, from whose lofty mizzen truck floated the broad blue pennant of the noblest sailor of them all, Rear Admiral Farragut, our glorious and beloved chieftain.

It was evident that something was brewing, and when, an hour later, the signal displayed from the *Hartford* read, "Commanding officers repair on board flagship"—all hands were on the alert, knowing the signal meant a war council. And when, a little later, the great monitor *Tecumseh* came steaming slowly up from the eastward, direct from New York, and anchored near the other ironclads, which had arrived the night before, we knew that the decisive moment, the moment for which we had been waiting so eagerly and long, was at hand.

About noon the captain of the *Lackawanna,* John B. Marchand, with which vessel I was then serving as assistant surgeon, returned, and one glance at his stern old face told us of coming strife. As he passed aft, he beckoned the executive officer, Lieutenant Thomas S. Spencer, and, after a moment's conversation, the latter came forward, his face all aglow with excitement as he said, "Tomorrow at daylight, fellows, hurrah!"

We had known for two weeks which ships were to participate, as they had been away to Pensacola navy yard, two at a time, for the purpose of stripping off all the spars and rigging which might interfere with their efficiency in action, and to have their sides covered, opposite the boilers and machinery, with a double casing of heavy chain cable, so as in some measure to ironclad them over their weakly-protected vitals.

Considerable delay had already been experienced in awaiting the arrival of the heavy monitors, without whose aid it was deemed unwise to attack the formidable ram *Tennessee,* of whose strength we only knew that the Rebel engineers called her the most powerful ever built, and no one had yet forgotten the *Atlanta* or the *Merrimac.* Admiral Farragut would have attacked without them, had they delayed another day, and the result of the action proved the correctness of his often-repeated assertion that "the same officers and men taken from an ironclad and put on board of a wooden ship, would give a better account of themselves, and have a better chance in the latter than in the former."

At noon on the fourth of August, the order of battle was sent on board the ships which were to participate, and the line formed: the *Brooklyn* and *Octorara*, the *Hartford* and *Metacomet*, the *Richmond* and *Port Royal*, the *Lacka-wanna* and *Seminole*, the *Monongahela* and *Kennebec*, the *Ossipee* and *Itasca*, the *Oneida* and *Galena*—and the four monitors—*Tecumseh, Manhattan, Winnebago* and *Chicka-saw*. The order read:

"Flagship *Hartford*
Off Mobile Bay, August 4, 1864.
The above diagram will be observed tomorrow morning, or when the fleet goes in.

D. G. Farragut, *Rear Admiral.*"

Then we knew that before twenty-four hours passed, we should either be inside Mobile Bay, conquerors of the stronghold and captors of the Rebel fleet, or be ourselves quietly at rest beneath its muddy waters. Yet one would have thought the busy preparation on every hand for some fete—some pleasure sail, so gay were officers and men. Many had left their valuables ashore at Pensacola to be forwarded to relatives in case of disaster—and now it only remained to while away the few remaining hours as best we might.

Scores of officers from the left-out ships came aboard to negotiate exchanges with some of the lucky ones, but not one man could be found who would trade and stay out. All were certain of success under our beloved chieftain, although we knew there was hot work ahead; for, as you will see by the diagram, we were to pass and did pass within eight hundred yards of Fort Morgan and its powerful water batteries upon which the Rebel engineers placed their main dependence, and which we had been informed mounted more than one hundred heavy guns.

Yet we clinked glasses merrily with our staybehind comrades and they bade us good night with envious faces cursing their luck—each one wishing that something might happen to one of the attacking fleet so that his own ship could have a chance in the fray.

Morning came at last after so busy a night that only an hour could be given to sleep. At eight bells or four o'clock all hands were turned out and our consort the *Seminole* steamed alongside and was made fast to us on the port side. The vessels were doublebanked in this manner in order that the farthest from the fort and protected from its fire might carry the other through should she either be disabled by shot or have her propeller entangled in any of the numerous floating ropes with which the Rebels had filled the channel for that express purpose.

The morning was beautifully clear and the battlements of Forts Morgan and Gaines with the few gaunt pines on Mobile Point stood out in clear relief against the blazing eastern sky all giving promise of a fine day. Later as is usually the result of heavy cannonading clouds came up and a slight shower occurred during the latter part of the action.

The *Brooklyn,* with the *Octorara,* steamed into position at the head of the line, and the other vessels fell in as soon as possible, at intervals of fifty yards. The flagship did not lead, because the *Brooklyn* was fitted with an ingenious contrivance to catch torpedoes, called a devil, composed of a number of long iron hooks attached to a spar, which was slung from the bowsprit and sunk even with the ship's keel, and for the further reason that her commander, Captain James Alden, knew the channel thoroughly, as he had been chief of the coast survey in antebellum days, and author of the official charts of the harbor.

At twenty minutes to six the line was formed, and we commenced to steam in slowly, the Admiral's order being to carry the lowest possible pressure, so as to avoid as much as possible the fearful scalding effect of the steam, should the boilers be pierced. The ships were dressed from stem to stern in flags, as if for a gala day, and every man sprang to his station with a will when the long roll called all hands to general quarters, which was sounded the moment we were fairly underway.

As the *Brooklyn* came within range of the fort, the Rebels opened the dance with a single gun, a 300-pounder Armstrong, at precisely seven o'clock.

It is a curious sight to watch a single shot from so heavy a piece of ordnance. First, you see the puff of white smoke upon the distant ramparts and then you see the shot coming, looking exactly as if some gigantic hand had thrown in play a ball toward you. By the time it is halfway, you get the boom of the report, and then the howl of the missile, which apparently grows so rapidly in size that every green hand on board who can see it is certain that it will hit him between the eyes. Then, as it goes past with a shriek like a thousand devils, the inclination to do reverence is so strong that it is almost impossible to resist it.

On board the *Lackawanna* we had several youngsters just from the Academy, and it was amusing to see how the nerves, which were as steel an hour later, gave way at first. Leaving their respective stations as the great shot drew near, they ran, fore and aft, bumped against one another in their efforts to get out of the way. The laughter of the older officers speedily recalled them to their senses, and they made good time back to their guns, which were none the less bravely fought for the momentary weakness. For half an hour, as we steamed up into range, the fleet took the entire Rebel fire without returning a gun, and the minutes seemed like hours.

But at last the signal came, "Commence firing," the cannonade grew furious, and the scene became terribly exciting and fascinating. It is difficult to explain to those who have never taken part in any closely contested battle, the complete loss of personal fear which occurs as soon as work fairly begins. Comrades are falling in every direction around you, yet no thought of danger enters one's brain and the only impulse is to kill as many of the enemy as possible —men are transformed into tigers.

The battle was a fair one, ships against brick walls and earthworks, each side doing its level best. As the fleet came into action, however, the broadsides came too fast and heavy for any mortal beings to stand, and the Rebel soldiers fled from the parapet in dismay. Shell, grape, and canister from the great cannon went hissing through the air, until it seemed as if hell itself had broken loose, and smoke was so dense on the decks and water that both fort and vessels were completely hidden and we both fired at the flashes of the guns alone.

Admiral Farragut, finding it impossible to see his ships from the deck so as to direct their movements, ascended the main rigging nearly to the top, whence he had a clear view, being above the smoke which lay so thick below. Captain Percival L. Drayton [of the *Hartford*], fearing that a chance shot might cut the shrouds and let the Admiral fall, sent a quartermaster aloft who passed one end of a signal halyard around the admiral and made him fast to the main-yard, so that there was no danger from that source. And Admiral Farragut was so completely absorbed in the fight that he did not discover what had been done until he came to descend after we had passed the forts.

The Rebels now opened from the guns of the water batteries, 8-inch guns and Armstrong rifles, which being on a level with the ships, did fearful execution. The *Mononga-hela* was struck many times, and Lieutenant Roderick Prentiss, her executive officer, had his right leg torn off by a whole shell, and Captain J. R. M. Mullany, of the *Oneida*, lost an arm in the same way. The latter vessel was struck by a heavy shell which, having penetrated completely through the chain armor and side of the vessel, exploded in her starboard boiler, instantly filling her engine and firerooms with steam. Every one of the fireroom gang was disabled, many being instantly killed by inhaling the vapor, and some of the bodies presented the ghastly spectacle of white bones from which the flesh had been stripped by the boiling steam. The vessel was disabled and was towed in by her consort, the *Galena,* nevertheless keeping her guns going steadily. A 200-pounder shell, on its upward ricochet from the water, struck the port sill of the *Lackawanna* under the 300-pounder rifle and killed and wounded one half of its crew, including Lieutenant S. A. McCarty, who was struck by a flying splinter and badly hurt. The shell then went overboard through the foremast without exploding. The other vessels got their fair share of attention from the enemy, but were not disabled.

The ram *Tennessee* started out from behind the fort just before the head of the line was abreast of it, intending to attack the fleet seriatim; but, receiving two or three broadsides, changed her course and ran back again, closely followed by the monitor *Tecumseh.* As the latter neared the fort, pounding away at the ram with 15-inch solid shot, she struck a floating cask torpedo and exploded it. As was afterwards ascertained by the divers, the explosion tore a hole in her bottom more than twenty feet square, and she sank like a stone—turning over as she went down in eight fathoms of water.

Commander Tunis A. M. Craven, one of the most gallant officers in the service, lost his life through his noble disregard of self. He was in the pilothouse with the pilot, close to the only opening in the whole ship, and this was only large enough to allow one man to pass at once. Captain Craven was already partly out, when the pilot grasped him by the leg, and cried, "Let me get out first, Captain, for God's sake; I have five little children!"

The Captain drew back, saying, "Go on, sir," gave him

his place, and went down with his ship, while the pilot was saved. [John Collins, the pilot, survived to relate his own version. Captain Craven, he recalled, conveyed this last order, "After you, pilot," while the two stood by the ladder.]

A week afterwards, when the divers went down to examine the wreck, they found nearly all the crew at their posts, as they sank. The chief engineer, who had been married in New York only two weeks before, and who had received from the flagship's mail his letters while the line was forming, stood with one hand upon the revolving bar of the turret engine, and in the other an open letter from his bride, which his dead eyes still seemed to be reading.

The shocking speed with which the *Tecumseh* went under caused the *Brooklyn,* still in the lead, to heave to. A lookout shouted back to the *Hartford:* "Torpedoes ahead!" It was then that Farragut screwed up his face and barked:

"Damn the torpedoes! Four bells! Captain Drayton, go ahead!"

By this time, the fleet was nearly past the forts, and the head of the line about crossing the middle ground, the ram still lying quietly under the guns of the fort. Cheer after cheer rent the air from hundreds of lusty throats, as the ships came, two by two, inside the bay, the goal we had been longing for so eagerly for three long years. Comrades shook hands, congratulated each other, and hurrahed until hoarse. The wounded were brought up from below and comfortably stowed away in cots, and the dead were decently composed for their long, last sleep, on the port side of the berth deck forward.

But all too soon; for another, and for us the hardest tug, was yet to come. Admiral Buchanan, in the *Tennessee,* had made up his mind to attack the whole fleet, and as her officers said afterwards, do his best and sink his ship with all hands or conquer. On she came, steadily and fast, paying no more attention to the terrible fire that was concentrated upon her from the entire fleet than to so many hailstones, and attempted to ram several of the large ships. Having cast loose from their consorts, they were too fast for her, and she did not manage to strike a single one.

Soon the monitors came up, and solid 11- and 15-inch shot struck her a dozen a minute from a range of less than a hundred yards without the slightest effect, she blazing away with her battery of 7-inch Brooks rifles. Never was ship more gallantly fought against more fearful odds. Finding what small impression our fire was making upon her, the Admiral now signaled the *Lackawanna, Monongahela,* and *Ossipee,* "Run down the Rebel ram." Four bells—"Go ahead, full speed"—rang from the bridge, the captain's post, and we went at her.

The *Monongahela* missed her aim the first time, striking obliquely a glancing blow with no harmful effect to either. The *Lackawanna* was more fortunate and delivered a fair blow, going at the tremendous speed of fourteen knots, just where the iron house joined the main deck, with a shock that prostrated every man on deck and tore to atoms her solid oak bow for six feet as if it had been paper. No more damage was done the ram by this tremendous blow than if a lady had laid her finger upon the iron sheathing, and a careful inspection of the spot where the contact occurred, made directly after the surrender, showed for the sole result a few oaken fibers forced directly into the iron.

The *Lackawanna* backed clear of the *Tennessee,* when the latter swung around on our port beam and delivered her broadside into us at three feet distance, at the same time receiving the fire of the only gun that could be sufficiently depressed to reach her, our deck being several feet higher out of water than hers. Her shell, 98-pounder percussion, all exploded on the berth deck, just as they entered the ship, entirely destroying the powder division, with the exception of the officer in command, Ensign Clarence Rathbone, who was wounded by flying splinters. The surgeon's steward and one nurse were torn into such small pieces that no part of either of them was ever identified.

The scene on the berth deck was dismal enough. So full of smoke that where a moment before was a crowd of busy men, nothing was visible except the red glare of the blazing woodwork which had taken fire from the exploding shell. With no sound beside the groans of the wounded and dying and the thunder of cannon overhead, a new element of horror was added by the news that the magazine was on fire! In that chamber were stored seventeen tons of gunpowder, and if the flames reached that, our shrift were short indeed.

In the magazine of a man-of-war, the powder is put up in cartridges of red flannel, of various sizes, and these are stored for greater safety in copper canisters, each containing about one hundred pounds. In passing up the cartridges to the boys whose duty it was to carry them to the guns, and who are called powder monkeys, the gunner had shaken out on the floor of the magazine passage a small quantity of powder which lay in little heaps along the passage, a long narrow way leading from the berth deck to the main chamber.

From one of these little heaps to another, and around the prostrate forms of the gunner, who had been stunned by the concussion, flame was flashing toward the deadly mass, when the ship's armorer, George Taylor, came at a leap down from the spar deck and, seeing at a glance the deadly peril, sprang down into the passage and extinguished the fire with his naked hands, burning them to the bone in the process—but saving all our lives and the brave old ship.

How many men would have had the pluck to go down into a magazine full of powder, a part of which was actually burning, and take the chances of being able to put it out with his naked hands is a problem which I leave you to solve. The gallant tar was publicly thanked the next day by Captain Marchand before the entire crew, and subsequently received the Medal of Honor which Congress voted for acts of special bravery.

Then the *Monongahela* returned to the attack and struck the ram fairly amidships, only injuring herself by the blow. The Rebel officers were astounded at the audacity of wooden ships attacking their vessel in this way, they expecting that the ironclads would alone dare to fight them. The ram [*Tennessee*] now stood away for the fort, followed by the whole fleet and almost covered with shot. Her smokestack was gone level with the deck, her steering gear, which, by some unaccountable stupidity, was rove on deck instead of below, was shot away, and, at ten o'clock precisely, she hauled down her colors and ran up the white flag, amidst thundering cheers from all hands of us and feelings of indescribable exultation.

Admiral Buchanan handed his sword to Lieutenant Giraud, temporarily of the *Ossipee,* who ran up the Stars and Stripes and carried the sword to the gallant Farragut on board the *Hartford.* Admiral Buchanan being wounded in the leg by a splinter [while himself serving one of his guns], the ship was given up by her executive officer, Commander James D. Johnston, with the assurance that if the officers had had their way, the ship would have been blown up before surrender; but that the men got wind of their intention and prevented it. [Only two were killed and eight wounded aboard the ram.]

During the latter part of the engagement, the *Metacomet,* under Lieutenant Commander James E. Jouett, chased the Rebel gunboat *Selma* up the bay, and, going two knots to her one, speedily overhauled her. After a running fight and the reception of two broadsides, Captain P. U. Murphy hauled down his colors and surrendered—himself wounded, his first lieutenant killed, and one-third of his crew *hors du combat.* The *Morgan* escaped up the bay to Mobile, and the *Gaines,* the last of Admiral Buchanan's fleet, was run ashore and set on fire by her crew, who then escaped into the woods.

Thus ended this glorious battle, with a glorious victory, the hardest fought naval engagement of the war, and, as was said by foreign critics, one of the fiercest on record. Indeed, it was the only one of the rebellion, except the duel of the *Kearsarge* and *Alabama,* when ships met ships fairly. It gave us entire possession of the harbor, cutting off the most available source of Rebel supply from abroad, capturing their famous ram and whole fleet, thereby proving the hollowness of Admiral Buchanan's boast "that he would sink every one of Farragut's ships or blow them out of water," and establishing the maxim that no shore fortifications, however strong, can stop the passage of a well-handled fleet of warships.

The spectacle of the naval engagement from shore was so superb that the troops, which were fighting at Fort Gaines, on Dauphin Island, suspended operations by mutual consent for two hours and watched the ships. About midnight the Rebels evacuated and blew up Fort Powell, giving us a clear passage to New Orleans via Mississippi Sound, and completely isolating Fort Gaines, which surrendered to Admiral Farragut the next day.

It was this gallant fight which, in the opinion of the "British Army and Navy Journal," the leading military authority in Europe, placed the noble Farragut at the head of the living naval commanders of the world and gave him equal fame with Nelson. Greater praise from Englishmen, there could be none.

It was wonderful to witness the courage of the men who were mortally wounded. One of our quarter-gunners who had both arms shot away above the elbows, and was supposed to be dead from the shock, astonished me by asking, while I was attending a man nearby, "Have we got in yet, sir?"

"Yes," I replied, "we have, thank God." "Then hurrah for our Admiral!" he exclaimed, and was dead in a moment afterward.

The next morning, the Admiral issued the following general order, which was read on board each ship while yet our dead were with us, and while the marks of the fight on every hand so powerfully emphasized the words:

"Flagship *Hartford*
Mobile Bay, August 6, 1864
"The Admiral returns thanks to the officers and crews of the Fleet for their gallant conduct during the fight. It has never been his good fortune to see men do their duty with more cheerfulness, for, although they knew the enemy was prepared with all devilish means for their destruction, and witnessed the almost instantaneous annihilation of our gallant companions in the *Tecumseh* by a torpedo, and the slaughter of their friends and messmates and gunmates, still there was not the slightest evidence of hesitation to follow your Commander-in-chief through the line of torpedoes and obstructions of which we knew nothing, except from the exaggerations of the enemy, 'that we would be blown up, as certainly as we attempted to enter.' For this blind confidence in your leader, he thanks you.

D. G. Farragut, *Rear Admiral.*"

—a paper by Passed Assistant Surgeon William F. Hutchinson, United States Navy, read before the Rhode Island Soldiers and Sailors Historical Society, October 4, 1876

◆◆◆ *The Federal squadron lost 145 killed, 93 of them on the* Tecumseh, *and 170 wounded. Twelve died and twenty were wounded among the Confederate naval defenders. "Davy" Farragut's wooden ships proved anew their ability to reel with the punches, sustaining slightly more than one hundred direct hits. The* Brooklyn *was hit thirty times, the* Hartford, *twenty. The* Metacomet, *with eleven individual shot and shell scars, was converted into a hospital ship to hasten the wounded of both sides to Pensacola hospitals.*

Fort Morgan, pummeled and battered by tons of shells from land and sea, including those from the captured Tennessee, *surrendered on August 23. The loss of strategic Mobile Bay, capped a week later by the fall of Atlanta, was a blow of incalculable severity to the Confederacy, portending as it did the bisecting of the South by Sherman's march to the sea and the ultimate capture of Richmond.*

Mobile itself, however, held out until after the surrender of Lee's armies at Appomattox, on the following April 10.

Dr. Hutchinson returned to the practice of medicine in Rhode Island, where he died in 1893.

No serious diving attempts were instituted until one hundred and three years after the battle when the Navy and the Smithsonian Institution located the wreck of the Tecumseh *and commenced salvage. An anchor, dining plates, and other tableware were recovered from the monitor's muddy resting place in fifty feet of water.*

No substantiation, however, could be found for Dr. Hutchinson's fanciful report of the chief engineer's clutching "an open letter from his bride." ◆◆◆

Hobson's Choice

◆◆◆ *The issues over which the Civil War was fought—intricate as they inherently were—appeared understandable, at least in a general way, to Rebel and Yankee alike. This was hardly the case with the Spanish-American War, which flamed into violence two months after the sinking of the* Maine *in Havana Harbor the night of February 15, 1898.*

Even after the relatively modern battleship was raised, several years later, the cause of the explosion that wrecked her and killed two hundred and sixty of those aboard was not conclusively determined. Nor was it at all clear that the United States had any right to aid the insurgents in seeking independence from their mother country, Spain.

However, Congress thought there was provocation enough for the conquest of Cuba and destruction of all Spanish naval flotillas found upon the high seas and in the world's harbors. On May 1, Admiral George Dewey, a veteran of Mobile Bay and other Civil War battles, made a fair start by quickly sinking Admiral Don Passaron's entire squadron of seven cruisers and some auxiliary vessels in Manila Bay.

77

The cost to the United States Navy was only eight wounded and superficial damage to the U.S.S. Olympia, *Dewey's flagship, and to the* Baltimore.

Two months later, Admiral William T. Sampson scored a repeat performance off Santiago Harbor, Cuba, by obliterating Admiral Pascual Cervera's squadron of four ancient armored cruisers and three destroyers, with upwards of five hundred casualties, mostly killed. Again, the battle was brief and the losses wholly disproportionate. One man only died, aboard the Brooklyn.

Neither naval engagement, since the fleets were so scandalously mismatched, was in the grand tradition of Trafalgar. However, one nautical episode of the war, in which every advantage was with the Spaniards, dwarfs all other operations for its sheer daring and imagination.

Since the commencement of hostilities, Cervera's pitiful assemblage of warships had been bottled up within the confines of Santiago Harbor. Embracing only eighteen square miles, the narrow anchorage was about one-twentieth the size of Mobile Bay.

One reason for Sampson's disproportionate watchdog squadrons was the groundless fear that the Spanish don would raid the East Coast of the United States. Cervera's very flagship, the Reina Mercedes, *built in the '80's, was reminiscent of some worn relic out of the Alcázar. Depending heavily on her supplemental yards of sail, she could steam along at a bare nine knots—exactly half the top cruising of Sampson's flagship,* New York.

In this tightly landlocked bay flanked by rugged promontories, however, the Spanish vessels were well protected by the guns of Morro Castle, off the entrance, Estrella Battery, and other forts perched atop the lofty commanding bluffs. Sampson's blockading fleet dared not steam within range. On the other hand, if the channel leading into the harbor—but three hundred and fifty feet wide in places— were to be closed, Cervera's ships could be picked off at leisure by invading artillery battalions and the United States' men-of-war put to use elsewhere.

Sampson's plan was to sink an old vessel in this channel. He found a willing volunteer in Lieutenant Richmond Pearson Hobson, twenty-eight-year old Alabaman and engineering graduate of Annapolis. The vessel chosen was the collier Merrimac, *which was almost as long as the channel at its narrowest width.*

Manned by Hobson and six other volunteers, the Merrimac, *loaded with ten torpedoes, a seemingly more than adequate scuttling charge, bid her silent adieus to the American blockaders on June 3—in bright moonlight—and thumped in slowly towards Morro Castle and the headlands before Santiago.*

Shortly after the Merrimac *had cast off, a seventh crewman appeared, introducing himself as Coxswain Randolph Clausen, twenty-eight years old. He was a stowaway, who explained he was afraid he would not have been accepted had he applied in customary fashion. There was nothing to do but muster him into ship's company.*

This is Hobson's own story: ◆◆◆

. . . a flash darted out from the water's edge at the left side of the entrance. The expected crash through the ship's side did not follow, nor did the projectile pass over; it must have gone astern. Strange to miss at such short range! Another flash—another miss! This time the projectile plainly passed astern.

Night-glasses on the spot revealed a dark object—a picket-boat with rapid-fire guns lying in the shadow. As sure as fate he was firing at our rudder, and we should be obliged to pass him broadside within a ship's length! If we only had had a rapid-fire gun we could have disposed of the miserable object in ten seconds; yet there he lay unmolested, firing point-blank at our exposed rudder, so vital to complete success. A flash of rage and exasperation passed over me. The admiration due this gallant little picket-boat did not come till afterward.

Glasses on the starboard bow showed the sharp, steep, step-like fall with which the western point of Morro drops into the water. This was the looked-for guide, the channel carrying deep water right up to the wall.

"A touch of port helm!" was the order.

"A touch of port helm, sir," was the response.

"Steady!"

"Steady, sir."

Now, even without helm, we should pass down safe. Suddenly there was a crash from the port side.

"The western battery has opened on us, sir!" called George Charette, who was still on the bridge, waiting to take the message to the engine-room if telegraph and signal-cord should be shot away.

"Very well; pay no attention to it," I replied, without turning, Morro Point, on the starboard side requiring all attention. The latter part of the answer was spoken for the benefit of the helmsman.

"Mind your helm!"

"Mind the helm, sir."

"Nothing to starboard?"

"Nothing to starboard, sir."

The clear, firm voice of Coxswain Oscar Deignan told that there need be no fear of his distraction. I estimated the distance to Morro Point at about three ships' lengths, and wondered if the men below would stand till we covered another ship's length, two ships' lengths being the distance at which it had been decided to give the signal to stop.

All of a sudden, *whir! cling!* came a projectile across the bridge and struck something. I looked. The engine telegraph was still there. Deignan and the binnacle were still standing. Two and a half ships' lengths! Two ships' lengths! Then over the engine telegraph went the order: "Stop."

Sure and steady the answer-pointer turned. There need have been no anxiety about the constancy of the brave men below.

The engine stopped.

"You may 'lay down' to your torpedoes now, Charette."

"Aye, aye, sir."

On the vessel forged, straight and sure the bow entered. Morro shut off the sky to the right. The firing now became general, but we were passing the crisis of navigation and could spare attention to nothing else. A swell seemed to set our stern to port, and the bow swung heavily toward Morro, which we had hugged close intentionally.

"Starboard!"

"Starboard, sir." Still we swung starboard!

"Starboard, I say!"

"The helm's astarboard, sir."

Our bow must have come within thirty feet of Morro rock before the vessel began to recover from the sheer, and we passed it close aboard.

"Meet her!"

"Meet her, sir."

The steering-gear was still ours, and only about half a ship's length more and we should be in the position chosen for the maneuver. The sky began to open up beyond Morro. There was the cove. Yes; there was the position! "Hard aport!"

"Hard aport, sir." No response of the ship!

"Hard aport, I say!"

"The helm is hard aport, sir, and lashed."

"Very well, Deignan," I said; "lay down to your torpedo."

Oh, heaven! Our steering gear was gone, shot away at the last moment, and we were charging forward straight down the channel!

We must have had four and three quarters knots' speed of our own, and the tide must have been fully a knot and a half. What ground-tackle could hold against a mass of over seven thousand tons moving with a velocity of six knots? We stood on a little longer to reduce the speed further. A pull on Murphy's cord to stand by—three steady pulls—the bow-anchor fell. A pause, then a shock, a muffled ring above the blast of guns: torpedo No. 1 had gone off promptly and surely, and I knew that the collision bulkhead was gone.

If the bow-chain in breaking would only give us a sheer and the other torpedoes proved as sure, we should have but a short interval to float, and holding on to the stern-anchor, letting go only at the last moment, we might still effectually block the channel. An interval elapsed and grew longer— no answer from torpedo No. 2, none from No. 3. Thereupon I crossed the bridge and shouted: "Fire all torpedoes!"

My voice was drowned. Again and again I yelled the order, with hands over mouth, directing the sound forward, below, aft.

It was useless. The rapid-fire and machine-gun batteries on Socapa slope [on the western shore of the channel] had opened up at full blast, and projectiles were exploding and clanging. For noise, it was Niagara magnified. Soon Charette came running up.

"Torpedoes 2 and 3 will not fire, sir; the cells are shattered all over the deck."

"Very well; lay down and underrun all the others, beginning at No. 4 and spring them as soon as possible."

In a moment No. 4 went off with a fine ring. Deignan had waited for No. 2 and No. 3, and not hearing them had tried his own, but had found the connections broken and the cells shattered. He then went down to Clausen at No. 5. No other torpedo responded. No. 6 and No. 8 had suffered the same fate as Nos. 2, 3, and 4. With only two exploded torpedoes we should be some time sinking, and the stern-anchor would be of first importance. I determined to go down aft and stand over to direct it personally, letting go at the opportune moment.

Passing along the starboard gangway, I reached the rendezvous. Stepping over the men, they appeared to be all present. There was Charette, returned from a second attempt at the torpedoes. There could be no further hope from that quarter, and, oh! there was Daniel Montague [Chief Master at Arms]! The stern-anchor, then, was already gone. If the chain was broken, we should have no further means of controlling our position.

Looking over the bulwarks, I saw that we were just in front of Estrella [behind Morro Castle], apparently motionless, lying about two thirds athwart the channel, the bow to the westward. Could it be that the ground-tackle had held? Then we should block the channel in spite of all. I watched, almost breathless, taking a range of the bow against the shoreline.

The bow moved, the stern moved—oh, heaven! the chains were gone! The tide was setting us down and would straighten us out if the stern should touch first. Oh, for the warheads to put her down at once! But we were helpless. I said nothing to Montague about having let go the stern-anchor—indeed, gave him no evidence of my chagrin—for he had been instructed that if no signal came from the bridge he should let go a short time after the torpedoes ceased going off; and, moreover, the signal-cord from the bridge had been broken.

There was nothing further to do but to accept the situation. We mustered, counting heads, and thought all were present; but we must have counted wrongly, for after a minute or two Francis Kelly [a water tender] came across the deck on all fours. He had done his duty below with promptness and precision, and had come on deck to stand by his torpedo. While putting on his life preserver a large projectile had exploded close at hand—he thought against the mainmast—and he had been thrown with violence on the deck, face down, his upper lip being cut away on the right side. He must have lain there some little time unconscious, and had got up completely dazed, without memory. He looked on one side and then the other, saw the engine-room hatch—the first object recognized—and, under the force of habit, started down it, but found the way blocked by water, which had risen up around the cylinders.

The sight of the water seemed to bring back memory, and soon the whole situation dawned upon him; he mounted again, and with heroic devotion went to his torpedo, only to find the cells and connections destroyed, when he started for the rendezvous. He had, indeed, brought his revolver-belt, so as to be in uniform, and adjusted it after reaching us.

We were now moving bodily onward with the tide, Estrella Point being just ahead of the starboard quarter. A blasting shock, a lift, a pull, a series of vibrations, and a mine exploded directly beneath us. My heart leaped with exultation.

"Lads, they are helping us!" I looked to see the deck break, but it still held. I looked over the side to see her settle at once, but the rate was only slightly increased. Then came the thought, could it be that the coal had deadened the shock and choked the breach, or had the breach been made just where we were already flooded? A sense of indescribable disappointment swept over me. I looked again: no encouragement. But ah! we had stopped. Estrella Point had caught us strong, and we were steadily sinking two thirds athwart. The work was done, and the rest was only a question of time. We could now turn our attention toward the course of action to be taken next.

Upon arriving at the rendezvous, I ordered that no man move till further orders, and repeated the order to Kelly when he arrived. The order had been obeyed without murmur. I then said to them:

"We will remain here, lads, till the moon sets. When it is dark we will go down the after-hatch, to the coal, where her stern will be left out of water. Some of us will come up and get the rifles and cartridges from the boat. We will remain inside all day, and tonight at ebbtide try to make our way to the squadron. If the enemy comes on board, we will remain quiet until he finds us, and will repel him. If he then turns artillery on the place where we are, we will swim out to points farther forward."

The deafening roar of artillery, however, came from the other side, just opposite our position. There were the rapid-fire guns of different calibers, the unmistakable Hotchkiss revolving cannon, the quick succession and pause of the Nordenfelt multi-barrel, and the tireless automatic gun. A deadly fire came from ahead, apparently from shipboard. These larger projectiles would enter, explode, and rake us; those passing over the spar-deck would apparently pass through the deckhouse, far enough away to cause them to explode just in front of us. All firing was at point-blank range, at a target that could hardly be missed, the Socapa batteries with plunging fire, the ships' batteries with horizontal fire. The striking projectiles and flying fragments produced a grinding sound, with a fine ring in it of steel on steel.

The deck vibrated heavily, and we felt the full effect, lying, as we were, full length on our faces. At each instant it seemed that certainly the next would bring a projectile among us. The impulse surged strong to get away from a place where remaining seemed death, and the men suggested taking to the boat and jumping overboard; but I knew that any object leaving the ship would be seen, and to be seen was certain death, and, therefore, I directed all to remain motionless. The test of discipline was severe, but not a man moved, not even when a projectile plunged into the boiler and a rush of steam came up the deck not far from where we lay. The men expected a boiler explosion, but accepted my assurance that it would be only a steam-escape.

While lying thus, a singular physiological phenomenon occurred. After a few minutes, one of the men asked for the canteen, saying that his lips had begun to parch; then another asked, then another, and it was passed about to all. Only a few minutes had elapsed when they all asked again, and I felt my own lips begin to parch and my mouth to get dry. It seemed very singular, so I felt my pulse, and found it entirely normal, and took account of the state of the nervous system. It was, if anything, more phlegmatic than usual, observation and reason taking account of the conditions without the participation of the emotions.

We must have remained thus for eight or ten minutes, while the guns fired ammunition as in a proving-ground test for speed. I was looking out of the chock, when it seemed that we were moving. A range was taken on the shore. Yes, the bow moved. Sunk deep, the tide was driving it on and straightening us out. My heart sank.

Why did not the admiral let us have the warheads! The tide wrenched us off Estrella, straightened us out, and set us right down the channel toward the part where its width increases. Though sinking fast, there still remained considerable freeboard, which would admit of our going some distance, and we were utterly helpless to hasten the sinking.

A great wave of disappointment set over me; it was anguish as intense as the exultation a few minutes before. On the tide set us, as straight as a pilot and tugboats could have guided. Socapa station fired two mines, but, alas! they missed us, and we approached the bight leading to Churruca Point to the right, and the bight cutting off Smith Cay from Socapa on the left, causing the enlargement of the channel. I saw with dismay that it was no longer possible to block completely. The *Merrimac* gave a premonitory lurch, then staggered to port in a deaththroe. The bow almost fell, it sank so rapidly.

We crossed the keel-line of a vessel removed a few hundred feet away, behind Socapa; it was the *Reina Mercedes*. Her bow torpedoes bore on us. Ah! to the right the *Pluton* was coming up from the bight, her torpedoes bearing. But, alas! cruiser and destroyer were both too late to help us. They were only in at the death.

The stricken vessel now reeled to port. Someone said: "She is going to turn over on us, sir," to which I replied: "No; she will right herself in sinking, and we shall be the last spot to go under." The firing suddenly ceased. The vessel lowered her head like a faithful animal, proudly aware of its sacrifice, bowed below the surface, and plunged forward. The stern rose and heeled heavily; it stood for a moment, shuddering, then started downward, righting as it went.

A great rush of water came up the gangway, seething and gurgling out of the deck. The mass was whirling from right to left "against the sun"; it seized us and threw us against the bulwarks, then over the rail. Two were swept forward as if by a momentary recession, and one was carried down into a coal-bunker—luckless Kelly. In a moment, however, with increased force, the water shot him up out of the same hole and swept him among us.

The bulwarks disappeared. A sweeping vortex whirled above. We charged about with casks, cans, and spars, the incomplete stripping having left quantities on the deck. The life-preservers stood us in good stead, preventing chests from being crushed, as well as buoying us on the surface; for spars came end on like battering-rams, and the sharp corners of tin cans struck us heavily.

The experience of being swept over the side was rather odd. The water lifted and threw me against the bulwarks, the rail striking my waist; the upper part of the body was bent out, the lower part and the legs being driven heavily against what seemed to be the plating underneath, which, singularly enough, appeared to open.

A football instinct came promptly, and I drew up my knees; but it seemed too late, and apparently they were being driven through the steel plate, a phenomenon that struck me as being most singular; yet there it was, and I wondered what the sensation would be like in having the legs carried

out on one side of the rail, and the body on the other, concluding that some embarrassment must be expected in
swimming without legs. The situation was apparently re-
lieved by the rail going down. Afterward Charette asked:

"Did those oilcans that were left just forward of us
trouble you also as we were swept out?"

Perhaps cans, and not steel plates, separated before my
kneecaps.

When we looked for the lifeboat we found that it had
been carried away. The catamaran was the largest piece of
floating debris; we assembled about it. The line suspending
it from the cargo-boom held and anchored us to the ship,
though barely long enough to reach the surface, causing the
raft to turn over and set us scrambling as the line came taut.

The firing had ceased. It was evident the enemy had not
seen us in the general mass of moving objects; but soon the
tide began to drift these away, and we were being left alone
with the catamaran. The men were directed to cling close in,
bodies below and only heads out, close under the edges, and
were directed not to speak above a whisper, for the destroyer was near at hand, and boats were passing near. We
mustered; all were present, and direction was given to remain as we were till further orders, for I was sure that in due
time after daylight a responsible officer would come out to
reconnoiter.

It was evident that we could not swim against the tide to
reach the entrance. Moreover, the shores were lined with
troops, and the small boats were looking for victims that
might escape from the vessel. The only chance lay in re-

maining undiscovered until the coming of the reconnoitering boat, to which, perhaps, we might surrender without being fired on.

The moon was now low. The shadow of Socapa fell over
us, and soon it was dark. The sunken vessel was bubbling up
its last lingering breath. The boats' crews looking for refu-
gees pulled closer, peering with lanterns, and again the discipline of the men was put to severe test, for time and again
it seemed that the boats would come up, and the impulse to
swim away was strong. A suggestion was made to cut the
line and let the catamaran drift away. This was also emphat-
ically forbidden, for we should thus miss the reconnoitering
boat and certainly fall into less responsible hands. Here, as
before, the men strictly obeyed orders, though the impulse
for safety was strong to the contrary, and *sauve-qui-peut*
would have been justifiable, if it is ever justifiable.

The air was chilly and the water positively cold. In less
than five minutes our teeth were chattering; so loud, indeed,
did they chatter that it seemed the destroyer or the boats
would hear. It was in marked contrast with the parched lips
of a few minutes before. In spite of their efforts, two of the
men soon began to cough, and it seemed that we should
surely be discovered. I worked my legs and body under the
raft for exercise, but, in spite of all, the shivers would come
and the teeth would chatter.

We remained there probably an hour. Frogs croaked up
the bight, and as dawn broke, the birds began to twitter and
chirp in the bushes and trees near at hand along the wooded
slopes. Day came bright and beautiful. It seemed that nature

disregarded man and went on the same, serene, peaceful, and unmoved. Man's strife appeared a discord, and his tragedy received no sympathy.

About daybreak a beautiful strain went up from a bugle at Punta Gorda battery. It was pitched at a high key, and rose and lingered, long drawn out, gentle and tremulous; it seemed as though an angel might be playing while looking down in tender pity. Could this be a Spanish bugle?

Broad daylight came. The sun spotted the mountaintops in the distance and glowed on Morro and Socapa heights. The destroyer got up anchor and drew back again up the bight. We were still undiscovered.

Someone now announced: "A steam-launch is heading for us, sir."

I looked around and found that a launch of large size, with the curtains aft drawn down, was coming from the bight around Smith Cay and heading straight for us. That must be the reconnoitering party. It swerved a little to the left as if to pass around us, giving no signs of having seen us. No one was visible on board, everybody apparently being kept below the rail. When it was about thirty yards off I hailed. The launch stopped as if frightened, and backed furiously.

A squad of riflemen filed out, and formed in a semicircle on the forecastle, and came to a "load," "ready," "aim."

A murmur passed about among my men: "They are going to shoot us."

A bitter thought flashed through my mind: "The miserable cowards! A brave nation will learn of this and call for an account."

But the volley did not follow. The aim must have been for caution only, and it was apparent that there must be an officer on board in control.

I called out in a strong voice to know if there was not an officer in the boat; if so, an American officer wished to speak with him with a view to surrendering himself and seamen as prisoners of war. The curtain was raised; an officer leaned out and waved his hand, and the rifles came down.

I struck out for the launch and climbed on board aft with the assistance of the officer, who, hours afterward, we learned was Admiral Cervera himself. With him were two other officers, his juniors. To him I surrendered myself and the men, taking off my revolver-belt, glasses, canteen, and life-preserver. The officers looked astonished at first, perhaps at the singular uniforms and the begrimed condition of us all, due to the fine coal and oil that came to the surface; then a current of kindness seemed to pass over them, and they exclaimed:

"Valiente!"

Then the launch steamed up to the catamaran, and the men climbed on board, the two who had been coughing being in the last stages of exhaustion and requiring to be lifted. We were prisoners in Spanish hands.

—*The Sinking of the Merrimac,*
by Richmond Pearson Hobson,
New York, The Century Co., 1899

♦♦♦ *The entire complement of the* Merrimac *was treated very well in Morro Castle. Although Hobson failed to*

*block the channel to Santiago, his exploit had the negative
effect of alerting Admiral Cervera to the dangers of a subsequent successful operation of the same nature. This inspired
his rash sally to sea in July and the annihilation of his fleet.*

*With the investment by land of Santiago, Hobson's little
"commando" band was exchanged. The brave young lieutenant returned to a hero's welcome and lecture tours in the
United States. He devoted his postwar interests to the fight
against narcotics' addiction. Curiously, he did not receive
the Medal of Honor until 1933—and then from another
naval enthusiast, President Franklin D. Roosevelt, who once
had considered applying for Annapolis. Hobson died four
years later.*

*Hobson did not have much choice, but there is some
doubt that the expression "Hobson's choice" actually arose
from this exploit off Santiago. The young lieutenant's daring, however, would furnish inspiration to successive gener-
ations of American boys and add another chapter in the nation's book of courage and ingenuity.* ◆◆◆

The *Emden*'s Last Fight

◆◆◆ *In August, 1914, came World War I. The small cruiser* Emden *had rewritten naval history those first two months of conflict as Imperial Germany tore at sea commerce, which was the economic jugular of Great Britain and her allies. Steaming furiously in the South Pacific and Indian Ocean —retracing much of the* Alabama's *old wake—covering 30,000 miles, the 3,200-ton vessel had captured or sunk twenty-four merchantmen, representing 100,000 tons, destroyed two enemy warships, and raided the important ports of Penang and Madras. Already legend in her own time,* Emden *was regarded with ever-mounting awe and respect by the sporting British.*

Her forty-one-year-old captain, Karl von Mueller, lean, blond, artistic, was among the last of warfare's cavaliers. Not only daring and skillful, he was also a humanitarian. To the wife of Captain Thomas Robinson of the British freighter Kabinga, *he bid "auf Wiedersehen!" as he gallantly turned the ship loose to find her way to the nearest port. Aboard were three hundred men and women, prisoners from other prizes of war. Mueller had not harmed a single pas-senger or crewman. On the other hand, he had caught the 3,050-ton Russian cruiser* Jemtchug *in Penang Harbor, Malaya, and blown her to bits with all three hundred and fifty naval personnel aboard. War was war—but it was for combatants, not civilians, by von Mueller's meticulously observed rules.*

His undoing was a raid upon the cable station on North Keeling, or Direction Island, in the Cocos Group, six hun-dred miles southwest of Java in the Indian Ocean. While a landing party from the Emden, *commanded by Hellmuth von Muecke, the First Officer, was ashore, destroying the station, the Australian cruiser, H.M.A.S.* Sydney, *boiled in over the horizon. She was twice the German's size and mounting 6-inchers, as opposed to her adversary's 4.1-inchers.*

The story of the ensuing clash, the morning of November 9, 1914 is told by (Lieutenant) Franz von Hohenzollern, cousin of Kaiser Wilhelm's, a twenty-three-year old lieuten-ant aboard the Emden: ◆◆◆

The *Emden* left at 9:30, with her masthead flags set, and steamed northwest.

The English cruiser, approaching the *Emden* at full speed, was at first thought to be the English light-cruiser *Newcastle,* as she had three funnels. This class is slightly su-perior to the *Emden* in speed and armament, but under fa-vourable circumstances we could have settled without very great loss or damage.

Right: America's first naval hero, Captain John Paul Jones. (*U.S. Navy Photo*)

Below: Anton Otto Fischer portrayed Jones's *Bonhomme Richard* and England's H.M.S. *Serapis* in fierce hand-to-hand combat. His ship crippled, Captain Jones was asked by his foe if his flag had been struck in surrender. In answer, the American thundered his now immortal battle cry: "Struck, sir? I have only begun to fight!" (*U.S. Navy Photo*)

Nelson's H.M.S. *Victory* at Portsmouth in 1828, etched by Edward W. Cooke. (*U.S. Navy Photo*)

Left: Admiral "Davy" Farragut painted by Arthur Conrad. At Mobile Bay in 1864 he scoffed at Rebel mines with the words: "Damn the torpedoes. Go ahead!" (*U.S. Navy Photo*)

Right: By tying smaller ships in tandem alongside larger consort steamers, Farragut guarded the Union squadron against gunfire from the enemy's forts and brought it into the bay, thus gaining Federal control of Mobile Bay. (*U.S. Bureau of Ships, Photo No. 19-N-9795 in the National Archives*)

The *Merrimac* aground off Estrella Point, Cuba, June, 1898, by H.F. Sprague. (*From "The Sinking of the Merrimac" by Naval Constructor Hobson*)

The *Maine,* whose sinking sparked the Spanish-American War, is raised in 1912. (*Records of the Office of the Chief of Engineers, Photo No. CN-2330 in the National Archives*)

H.M.S. *Invincible,* which helped sink a German squadron, 1914.
(*U.S. Navy Photo*)

H.M.S. *Southampton* survived Jutland in 1916 in spite of incredible damage. (*U.S. Navy Photo*)

U. S. S. HELENA

Admiral Graf Spee

MAR 28 1940

PICTURES TAKEN 2 FEBRUARY 1940 by Ensign Sampson
U.S.S. HELENA SHAKEDOWN.

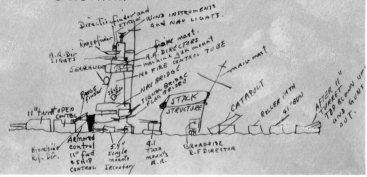

Above: Germany's *Admiral Graf Spee* was scuttled in December, 1939. Compelled to leave sanctuary after her running duel with British warships, the German captain chose self-destruction over surrender and blew up his ship in the River Plate estuary. (*U.S. Navy Photo*)

Left: Half submerged in shallow water six miles southwest of Montevideo, the *Graf Spee* was photographed and diagramed two months later by U.S.N. Ensign Sampson. The 10,000-ton pocket battleship sank nine British craft in three months before her own demise. (*U.S. Navy Photo*)

The carrier *Lexington* paid a high price for stopping the Japanese in May, 1942, at the Coral Sea, the first naval battle ever fought between surface units with no visual contact. The Japanese defeat, checking further invasion south, was a turning point of the war. The *Lexington,* doomed by severe fires from internal explosions, was abandoned and sunk. U.S.S. *Phelps* fired scuttling torpedoes to prevent her being salvaged by the enemy. (*U.S. Navy, Photo No. 80-G-7403 in the National Archives*)

At 9:35 the Englishman turned to starboard, forcing us into a running fight. The wind was favourable to us.

Five minutes later the range had narrowed from 13,000 to 10,000 yards. Von Mueller now gave the order to "open fire!" Thus, *Emden,* in spite of her inferiority in speed, opened the fight. Our opponent was the faster, and had also steam up in all boilers, whereas we had only a short time ago begun to get steam up in all boilers, and it would be a quarter of an hour before we could get steam in the engines for full speed.

We had hardly opened fire when the Englishman began to shoot, using for ranging purposes the fore and after guns, which confirmed us in the belief that our opponent was *Newcastle.*

Our first two salvoes went over, and the third as well, except for one hit that carried away the Englishman's range-finder and all his gear. The next shots were short at first, but then correct. In order to allow our 4.1-inch guns to work more effectively, the Captain turned two points to starboard after the first salvoes.

At 9:35 he again turned two points to starboard.

In the beginning the Englishman shot badly. Seven or eight salvoes were a great hindrance to our observation, as the splashes continually came over the ship, obscuring our glasses, and rendering observation very difficult.

From the columns of water thrown up by the shells we realized that they were all of the same bore, namely 5.9 inch [or 6 inch]. It was therefore clear that our opponent could not be a ship of the *Newcastle* class, but a modern cruiser.

The swell, now that we were out of the shelter of the island, was very noticeable.

After the *Emden*'s eighth salvo there was a fire in the enemy cruiser, caused by one of our shells which had gone into a store of ammunition and set it alight. Unfortunately this explosion did not do any great or decisive damage.

Our gunlayers shot very well. If we had had bigger bored guns the fight would at least have been more favourable for us.

Fairly soon the enemy's guns got into their stride, and the first enemy hits found the *Emden* after ten o'clock. The first hit struck the wireless cabin, which disappeared completely. Its remains were dust and ashes. The men on duty in it were killed outright.

The second exploded near the conning tower, between the foremast and the after side of the forecastle. One of the splinters hit the helmsman in the left forearm, and wounded him severely. The arm, however, was quickly bound up, and the helmsman continued his duties.

Almost at the same time a shell landed just forward of the conning tower with very considerable effect. The gun crews on the forecastle were disabled, along with some signalmen. Unfortunately no help could be brought to the wounded, as the first-aid party was fully occupied elsewhere, and the rest of the ship's company so tied to their posts that they could not leave them.

Now that the Englishman was shooting well, hit after hit drove home on our poor ship. Almost every minute, news reached the conning tower of a disablement at a gun, or some place near one.

Soon afterwards the electric transmitters for the guns failed, which proved a great hindrance. The gunnery officer had now to pass his orders through the speaking tubes, which had, however, also been hit, so that it was very difficult to convey orders. The natural consequence was that the battery shooting, which up to now had been coordinated, became irregular, and rendered observation difficult. Effective shooting, that is, shooting which would check the enemy, was no longer to be thought of.

The enemy now had command of the situation. With his advantage in guns and speed he could carefully range us without running any danger of really damaging hits from us. From the beginning our disadvantage was our weaker armament. For our 4.1-in. guns the highest range at which effective shooting could be carried out was 7,600–8,700 yards. If our opponent maintained a greater distance effective shooting was no more to be thought of, whereas the enemy, with 5.9-in. guns, could destroy us completely.

Further casualties were reported, and then both safeguards of our electric lighting were shot away. The steering telegraph and the steering gear in the conning tower both broke down, as the leads had probably been destroyed somewhere. The ship was now steered from the steering flat, and the engine-room telegraph was worked from the midships flat. Marine engineer Andresen was in command in the midships flat, and he also commanded the caulking party from there—really the post of the First Officer. As Lieutenant Commander von Muecke was ashore with the landing party at Direction Island, however, Andresen was representing him at this very important station.

Some minutes later the foremost funnel received a full hit, which threw it over to port. This was damaging for us as the smoke could not be drawn off properly. This had a retarding effect on the speed, since the fire in the furnace could not obtain enough air. Sufficient heat could not be produced or steam raised for full speed.

The *Emden*'s speed, at best lower than that of the enemy, was still further reduced.

Owing to the continuous hail of shells the losses in the guns' and magazines' crews were so severe that the guns could hardly be manned. Our guns, however, still shot with astonishing exactness and speed, but this could not last for long.

Lack of ammunition would be felt any minute. In fact the fire began to drop off slowly, and only a few guns were occasionally in action. The guns themselves were intact, but the munition hoists were mostly shot away, so that only after great efforts could ammunition be got up on deck.

It was necessary to operate everything manually, and therefore a large number of men were needed for the transport of munitions alone. As these men had to carry on their work unprotected the losses were terribly severe. There were no more reserves, and it would not be long before there were no more men for the guns and ammunition-carrying.

The third hit did the most damage, as it caught the ammunition placed ready at the fourth port gun, exploded it and killed and burned in the fearful flames all the men nearby. Anything inflammable caught fire, so that after this hit the whole after part of the ship was in flames.

Meanwhile there were more severe losses. The port guns also became silent one after another, for lack of personnel.

When von Mueller saw that the guns had been put out of action he tried, as the *Emden*'s last hope, to get near enough to the enemy to be able to try a torpedo. It was at this moment that we in the torpedo flat had received the order: "Starboard tube, ready!"

The time was 10:25. Unfortunately it was impossible to fire the torpedo, since the speed of the enemy, which at times attained 27 knots, prevented us from getting within torpedo range. The distance was for the most part 7,600 yards, and to put in an effective shot we had to get within 1,100 yards.

Our speed was low, and further reduced by the destruction of the funnel and insufficient steam. The rudder was not answering at all, and maneuvering with the screws took away a great deal of power, which still further reduced our speed.

During the maneuver for torpedo range the enemy had again got on to our starboard side. Our guns were now almost silent. Only now and then was a single shot fired.

Suddenly the Englishman turned to port and fired a torpedo at us (the time was 10:35). The range at the time was something more than 3,200 yards. The Englishman, with his modern torpedo weapons could also fire at greater range, though 3,200 yards is very long for a torpedo. We had time to evade the torpedo.

The whole thing was now only a game for the enemy. The guns of the *Emden* no longer threatened, and the Englishman avoided a torpedo by steering a zigzag course (our torpedo weapons were still intact). Finally the enemy turned to starboard and steamed away at high speed.

Shortly afterwards our gunnery officer left the conning tower, as control from there had become impossible. He tried to get up a constant stream of fire again by bringing together all the survivors of the gun crews and taking control himself from near the guns. He succeeded in manning two, but the effect of this last attempt was almost nothing, for the enemy kept at a safe distance and maintained a steady fire on the vanquished *Emden*.

There was not a single man who served his gun in fear of death. The faithfulness and heroism of these men was most evident. The heroes kept their posts to the bitter end. Several worked imperturbably in spite of severe wounds, among them a boatswain's mate who had had his right arm shot away. This warrior continued to load with the arm remaining to him, as if nothing had happened.

At about 10:50 the steering gear again broke down, and the navigating officer and a few men rushed aft to get to the hand-steering. Nothing, however, answered, and when this had been reported to the conning tower, steering was carried on by means of the ship's screws. Through this breakdown the *Emden* had made a turn hard a-starboard, so that the enemy could now rake our port side.

This change was very unpleasant for us, as the enemy got in three full hits which did a great deal of damage. The first landed near the bridge, shot away our range-finding gear, and killed the people on duty there. The second hit killed the remaining men at the guns forward of the conning tower, some of whom were already severely wounded.

Another hit wrecked the captain's bridge. In addition, our guns were now completely silenced, from which it was certain that our gunnery officer must be mortally wounded. Before, however, our Captain completely gave up the fight, he wished to make another attempt to get within torpedo range.

This maneuver was rendered more difficult by the fact that the communications between the conning tower and the starboard engines had failed, and all orders had to be passed by a gunnery transmitterman, who called the orders down the engine-room skylight. In spite of the hail of shells orders were passed regularly, and the seaman concerned was not even slightly wounded.

This last attempt to attain some positive success against the enemy was a complete failure, as the Englishman steered clear of every attempt to approach her, and kept at a respectful distance from our torpedoes.

In this maneuver also both the remaining funnels were shot away, so that our already slow speed was reduced to a minimum. That meant the end for us, for what had we left to fight with? Guns and torpedoes were both rendered useless by the failure of our speed.

This was the moment at which the Captain decided to run the *Emden* onto the coral reefs of North Keeling Island, hoping for two great advantages. First, the *Emden* would not fall into enemy hands, and, second, a number of lives would be saved. If the ship were to sink, a large number of the men, who had action stations under the armoured deck, and also all the severely wounded, would certainly be drowned without hope of rescue.

In order to put this operation properly into effect the starboard engines were stopped for a time, and we then ran straight for the island. The enemy had scarcely recognized our intention when he tried to sink us by an increased rate of fire, and crossed our bows in the hope of cutting off our way to the island. There was now an absolute hail of hits, but, thank God, the *Emden* remained seaworthy in spite of them. Many more of our men lost their lives at this point.

The Englishman wished to destroy us completely before we could run aground. He doubtless wanted to enjoy the triumph of seeing the *Emden* vanish into the depths, but this was denied him. When he saw that our ship was not hindered in her run for the island he had to give us room whether he wanted to or not, as otherwise he was in danger of being rammed.

Shortly before we ran aground a report reached the conning tower that a shell had pierced the armoured deck on the starboard side above the torpedo flat, and that the flat would have to be abandoned owing to danger from gas and water.

At 11:15 the *Emden,* with her engines stopped, ran on to the south coast, in this case the lee side, of North Keeling. The engines were again put to "full speed ahead," so that the cruiser might be firmly impaled on the coral reef. The engines were then stopped, fires drawn and seacocks opened. Our gallant *Emden,* in whom we had achieved so much success, was thus a complete wreck.

We now lay there quite unarmed, but the English ship continued her fire for another five minutes. Only at 11:20 did she cease fire.

This continued shooting at a wreck prompted our Captain to give the ship's company permission to jump overboard and try to reach the island, about 100 yards distant, by swimming. This was not easy, as there was a strong surf over the coral reef.

—*Emden,* by Franz Joseph, Prince of Hohenzollern,
G. Howard Watt, New York, 1928

◆◆◆ *A total of 134 of the* Emden's *complement had been killed or were drowned, while 65 were wounded, out of 355 aboard. This left only 117 unhurt since von Muecke's raiding party ashore numbered 50, including himself. In commandeered sailing vessels and by overland treks across the Arabian desert, von Muecke's sailors effected an incredible flight to freedom, finally arriving in Constantinople six months later. They lost only eight of their number to disease and in fights against tribesmen.*

The other survivors of the Emden *finished out the war in various British and Australian prison camps. Von Mueller was married shortly after the armistice and became the father of two daughters. Elected to the Brunswick Diet, a provincial legislature, the one-time cruiser commander was among those loyal Germans who tried hard to make the Weimar Republic work. He did not live to see its failure but died of pneumonia in 1923, a decade before a ruler far more aggressive than the Kaiser would again set Germany on the path of war.* ◆◆◆

Requiem for a Squadron

◆◆◆ *As in all massive wars, the fortunes of both sides in World War I seesawed continually. The fiery end of the* Emden *by no means implied that the British, the Australians, or others of the* Entente *were invariably winners—far from it.*

On September 22, 1914, for example, when the war was still so new that the combatants were imperfectly accustomed to it, the proud Royal Navy sustained an unprecedented defeat in the sinking of three 12,000-ton cruisers, the Aboukir, Cressy, *and* Hogue, *in the North Sea by a small, lone submarine, the U-9. With them went down more than 1,400 men, mostly reservists.*

Two months later, on Nobember 1, an entire British squadron was sunk or dispersed off Coronel, Chile. Lost were the cruisers Good Hope *and* Monmouth—*over 24,000 tons, combined—with their commander, Admiral Sir Christopher Cradock, and all hands. The smaller* Glasgow *fled in the approaching darkness, while the slow auxiliary, the converted liner* Otranto, *had never joined in the engagement upon these inhospitable Pacific waters.*

The triumph belonged to Admiral Graf Maximilian von Spee, whose own powerful squadron was built around the 11,000-ton heavy cruisers Scharnhorst *and* Gneisenau, *and the 3,300-ton light cruisers* Leipzig, Dresden, *and* Nürnberg.

Actually, it was an empty victory for Graf von Spee, far from any secure base, always uncertain of his next coaling stop, trying somehow to plow homeward. But in London, the loss of the warships with more than 1,600 officers and men was rightfully regarded as unmitigated tragedy. And something would *be done about it, even if the war had to be temporarily halted on every other front!*

First Lord of the Admiralty Winston Churchill and the explosive-tempered Admiral of the British Fleet, Sir John Fisher, at once assembled a "revenge" squadron led by the 17,000-ton battle cruisers Invincible *and* Inflexible, *mounting main batteries of 12-inch guns (contrasted with the* Scharnhorst's *8.1 inch) and capable of speeds approaching thirty knots. Chosen to command was a bulldog-jawed officer, Vice Admiral Sir Frederick Charles Doveton Sturdee.*

On November 10, the squadron was plowing southwestward, aiming at the lonely Falkland Islands—on the fringe of Antarctica and two hundred and fifty miles from Patagonia on the east coast of South America. Inhabited by a few hundred sheep raisers, the Falklands were among His Majesty's most southerly possessions.

On December 7, the Invincible *and the* Inflexible, *accompanied now by six smaller cruisers, dropped anchor at*

*Port Stanley, the only major place of habitation on the Falk-
lands. Unfortunately for him, Admiral von Spee was also
nearing these islands, for the dual purpose of coaling and of
destroying cables and anything else that might serve the purposes of his English foe.*

*The subsequent account is taken from the memoirs of a
thirty-three-year-old lieutenant commander aboard the* Invincible, *Edward Barry Bingham, an Irishman and a notable
polo player. He wrote:* ◆◆◆

At the first sign of dawn next morning, coaling began in
all ships of the squadron, other than the *Bristol* and *Glasgow,* who had completed the previous evening. The *Kent*
took up the position of guardship outside the harbour of Port
William. Two hours' work in the *Invincible* and *Inflexible*
yielded some 400 tons each. Then came an interval for a
well-earned breakfast. The third-cup-of-coffee-and-marma-
lade stage was being reached when a signalman dashed down
to the ward-room and, with praiseworthy efforts to preserve
his official calm, reported that one of the shore signal stations, Sapper Hill, had sighted two foreign men-of-war. In a
few minutes the news was confirmed and three more ships
were reported to the southward. Next they were finally
identified as being the German China Squadron. In truth
here was Admiral von Spee and his squadron steaming right
into the jaws of the lion.

Out of touch by wireless since he left Valparaiso, von
Spee had dawdled down the coast and round the Cape to the
Falklands, never dreaming for an instant that two powerful
battle-cruisers had been detached with the special object of

meeting him. His intentions were to do battle with such British force as he might encounter and to plunder the settlement; and indeed he was perfectly justified in thinking that he could beat any fair-sized combination of our older cruisers.

Amidst loud cheers the captain gave the order to "cast off colliers." Then followed the thrilling notes of the bugle call, "Action." At the same time the whole squadron was ordered to raise steam for full speed with all despatch. As guardship, the *Kent* had steam up, and this cruiser was directed to observe and report the enemy's movements. For all we knew the enemy might form up outside the harbour and enfilade us whilst we were raising steam at anchor. Had this plan of action entered his head things might have gone badly for those inside.

What we did not anticipate and only learned afterwards by personal experience was that the German guns were sighted up to 16,500 yards. Their range-finding, too, was admirable, and their gunnery control, as illustrated by the rippling salvoes, worked like clockwork. The only flaw in this otherwise perfect machine lay in the fact that the guns were if anything too well calibrated without sufficiency of spread, for straddling purposes; an instructive lesson that we were not slow to turn to account. The three remaining ships do not call for any additional comment, although attention should be drawn to the high speed of the *Dresden*.

When within fifteen miles of the Falklands, von Spee, who was flying his flag in the *Scharnhorst,* sent the *Gneisenau* and *Nürnberg* ahead to a distance of less than six miles from the harbour for the purpose of reconnoitring, while he himself, with the other ships, remained approximately eight miles off. According to the statement made subsequently by prisoners from the *Gneisenau,* it appears that the sub-lieutenant who had been sent aloft with powerful glasses to ascertain what British ships were in the harbour reported to his captain that there were two battle-cruisers and five other cruisers anchored there.

Such a statement sounded absolutely incredible to the captain, until a senior lieutenant, the gunnery officer, who was next sent up, confirmed the first report. The presence of dreadnought cruisers was thus placed beyond all doubt, and the fact could only be explained on the assumption of their being Japanese battle-cruisers; and here is to be found the explanation of the myth industriously circulated by the English press, to the effect that Japanese ships were present at the Battle of the Falkland Islands.

In any case, the enemy had an unwelcome surprise. It was for the *Gneisenau* to receive the second unpleasant shock when a report was heard and two 12-inch shells, about 9:20 A.M., dropped quite close to her, apparently from nowhere, but in reality the result of indirect fire from the *Canopus,* who lay obscured from seaward by an intervening hill. Controlled from a D.P.F. erected ashore, the *Canopus'* guns fired one more salvo of three shells. This bombardment the Germans imagined to come from a concealed land battery and thus received their third surprise. To experience three such shocks at a comparatively early hour, was something altogether too much for them. Von Spee recalled his two ships, and the whole squadron promptly took to their heels at maximum speed—probably about 21 knots—and steered in an easterly direction. They were closely shadowed by the *Kent,* who remained at a suitable distance and reported their movements, until the fleet had steam up and could chase their quarry.

Exactly an hour and a half after the order to raise steam, we were tearing out of the harbour and after the enemy, who had altered to S.E. To have raised steam in this short time from cold boilers argues remarkably fine work on the part of the engine-room staff; who, it need not be added, exposed their machinery to grave risks in taking ninety minutes to do that for which four hours is the usual allowance. It is pleasant to record that their efforts were specially mentioned in despatches and duly received recognition from the authorities at home.

It was 9:45 when we left the harbour on a glorious morning with a bright sun, almost dead calm and the clearest atmosphere. So great was the visibility, that on clearing the entrance of the harbour we were able at once to take the range of the enemy, the tops of whose masts and funnels were just above the horizon. The distance was found to be 38,000 yards, *i.e.* nineteen sea miles, or nearly twenty-two land miles.

From the previous description of the British ships it will be obvious that we could reckon on arriving within gun range (16,500 yards) in somewhat over four hours.

Almost immediately the *Bristol* and *Otranto* were detached to round up two ships which, reported by the volunteer signal stations as enemy's transports, turned out to be German colliers. The *Bristol* was at six hours' notice for steam, and by the time she had finished rounding up the colliers it was then too late to take any part in the action. With plenty of time before us, we had a rough-and-ready clean down of the ship from the coal dust, thoroughly tuned up the fighting machine, and sent the men to their dinners.

With their superior speed, the two battle-cruisers rapidly forged ahead of the older ships; and then, easing down at 11:15 o'clock, waited for the others to close up. Admiral Sturdee, however, in order not to lose the advantage of the fine weather conditions, cracked on once more about 12:20, working up to 25 knots or more. Fully convinced that our lighter craft could deal with them, he ignored the presence of the smaller German cruisers, and his sole determination was to force an action on the *Scharnhorst* and *Gneisenau* as soon as possible.

From this moment, then, the Battle of Falkland Islands may be described as an action—or rather, series of actions —in which big ships were opposed to big ships, and small cruiser pitted against small cruiser.

Soon after 1 o'clock, at a range of 17,000 yards, "A" turret (under my charge) got the order to fire a sighting shot at the *Leipzig*, the enemy's rear cruiser. Giving the guns their maximum elevation, I fired; and the result was short. The next round, fired at a distance of about 16,500 yards, nearly hit the *Leipzig*, who thereupon turned away with *Nürnberg* and *Dresden* to the S.W. These light cruisers were at once followed by *Glasgow*, *Kent*, and *Cornwall*. The fire of the *Invincible* and *Inflexible* was then directed on the *Scharnhorst*, who rapidly came into range.

The effect of this was that the *Scharnhorst* turned eight points to port—in other words, took a right-angled turn to the left. We followed suit, and thus, at 1:30, on parallel courses and at a distance of 16,000 yards, the action between the two pairs of large cruisers commenced.

During the outward voyage the opinion generally expressed was: first, that our Admiral intended fighting the action at a range of about 14,000 yards; and secondly, that this distance was beyond the range of the *Scharnhorst* and *Gneisenau*. But while right in one part of the conjecture, all were at fault in the corollary, for the truth was that the German salvoes were good for at least 16,500 yards, *i.e.* our own maximum range. Still, if in respect of maximum range there was nothing to choose between the opposing fleets, our guns with a lower trajectory and more M.V. [muzzle velocity] had a correspondingly greater danger-space; or otherwise expressed, the German shells fell almost vertically at that range, whilst ours travelled nearer the horizontal.

Hence a long-range action, even at a distance greater than that originally anticipated, was all in our favor.

Conversely, an action at close quarters would have exposed the two battle-cruisers to the risk of being hit in a vital spot by shell or torpedo; and if they were not actually sunk, it is obvious that with no dock nearer than Gibraltar—some 6,000 miles away—any large or serious repairs would have been out of the question.

The range was therefore kept long, and the ships zig-zagged from time to time when the enemy had gauged our range too successfully.

The action began at 1:30. Within a few minutes the *Scharnhorst* and *Gneisenau,* who were obviously concentrating on the *Invincible,* made a good start by hitting us at

1:45 with their third salvo. We then sheered off a couple of points, thereby throwing the Germans off their range, and the *Inflexible* followed our motions. The fire then opened rather rapidly, and the enemy at 2:10 made an attempt to get away by turning ten points to starboard. This caused a lull in the action from 2:15 until 2:45.

At 2:45 we again opened fire on them; the enemy replied at 2:55. From now until 3:15 P.M. the fighting was very fierce, the range decreasing to 10,000 yards. Both the *Scharnhorst* and *Gneisenau* were hit several times. The *Scharnhorst,* on fire forward, slackened her rate of fire, and accurate shooting was not maintained.

Between 3:15 and 3:30 our ship was so hampered by funnel and gun smoke that Admiral Sturdee was obliged to turn his ships in a complete circle to rid himself of this nuisance. The *Scharnhorst,* seeing this turn, made a fresh attempt to withdraw from the action, or perhaps it was to bring her other broadside into action; in any case she turned ten points away from us. However, once clear of smoke, we with our superior speed drew up into gun range, and fighting recommenced with all its former vigour.

From 3:30 onwards the *Scharnhorst* was being badly hit; it was noticed that in many parts of the hull fires were breaking out, and that two of the four funnels were missing. With this came an encouraging message from the captain, who told me down the voice-pipe that my turret was hitting well; personally I had observed two well-placed shots land successively just above the water-line, abreast of where the second funnel ought to have been.

At first I found it a little difficult to differentiate between the flash of the enemy's guns and one's own hits, but observation soon enlightened me on the fact that when you really strike home on a ship you see a little red glow, or in the case of lyddite a cloud of yellow smoke, suddenly appears.

Admiral Sturdee reported that notwithstanding the punishment the *Scharnhorst* was receiving, her fire was steady and accurate, and the persistency of her salvoes was remarkable. At 3:50 P.M. the German flagship was looking pretty sickly; practically motionless, fires everywhere, and only one funnel still standing. Finally, at 4:04 P.M., she rolled quietly over on one side, lay on her beam ends, and took a headlong dive, bows first, at 4:17 P.M.

This news I conveyed to my men in the four different chambers of the turret by means of the voice-pipe, and through the same channel could be heard the echoes of the cheering that rose from the very bowels of the ship. In a modern naval action, where all men are well down under armour, those who actually witness events do not amount to more than two score out of a complement of 990, and of a turret's crew of forty only four actually see the fight, viz. the two gunlayers, the turret trainer, and the range-taker, the remainder being distributed in the gun-house, the working chamber, the magazine and shell-room.

The *Gneisenau,* who had been following the *Scharnhorst,* continued to concentrate her fire on us, leaving to their fate any possible survivors from her sister ship. Under the circumstances any life-saving was out of the question, and not a soul from the *Scharnhorst* survived.

Now pitted against the *Inflexible* and ourselves, the solitary *Gneisenau* fought a losing fight for nearly two hours.

Admiral Sturdee in his report says: "At 4:47 the *Gneisenau* was hit severely. At 5:08 P.M. she was evidently in serious straits, and her fire slackened very much. Three ships—*Invincible, Inflexible, Carnarvon*—were concentrating on her from different bearings. At 5:15 she hit the *Invincible;* this was her last effective effort."

At 5:30 P.M. she was scarcely moving, with two funnels gone and several fires ablaze. A quarter of an hour later the *Gneisenau* stopped firing, having expended all ammunition, including even practice projectiles.

Almost on the stroke of 6 o'clock the *Gneisenau* rolled over and dived down in precisely the same way as her sister before her.

The survivors, running over the uppermost side, threw themselves into the water, while the British ships steamed up at full speed to the spot, a few minutes ago the cradle of a proud ship, and now only marked by oil, wreckage, and masses of struggling humanity. Every available boat was lowered, and while the *Invincible* and *Inflexible* each picked up 108 and sixty-two survivors respectively, the *Carnarvon* —who had by now joined up—saved twenty. The survivors included the commander of the *Gneisenau* and about fifteen officers.

I went away in one of the cutters and succeeded in picking up about forty survivors, most of them in a wounded condition, and all in various stages of exhaustion; and small wonder! for the ship in her last stages must have been a very hell on earth. Anyhow, it was a gruesome business for the rescuers.

A word must now be said about the doings of the smaller

cruisers, who had been left behind when the battle-cruisers made their final spurt after the *Scharnhorst* and *Gneisenau*. But as the *Bristol* and *Otranto* have already been dealt with, their remain only the *Kent, Glasgow,* and *Cornwall*.

These three confined themselves to chasing the enemy's three light cruisers which we left steaming to the S.W. More specifically, the *Glasgow* and *Cornwall* hunted the *Leipzig,* the *Kent* chased the *Nürnberg,* while with the advantages of speed and a good start, the *Dresden* got clear away.

Very different was the fate of the *Leipzig* and *Nürnberg,* who were both sunk with colours flying, after a stern chase and gallant resistance, which in the case of the latter was prolonged until the last moment of daylight.

Probably the *Kent* had reason to be most proud of herself on account of an extraordinary feat performed by her engine-room staff, who managed to get 23 knots out of a 22-knot ship that had been serving thirteen years.

The captain's racy account, as he gave it to me a few days later, of what they did and how they did it, deserves to be quoted in full: "We sat on the safety valves and forced the boilers fit to bust. We ran short of coal, so we burnt any spare wood left in the ship. About 6 P.M. we got within range. The *Nürnberg* started hitting us before we could hit her, so we went at it hammer and tongs. When it was getting dark, I closed in between two and three hundred yards. This paid me very well, because I had 6-in. guns against his 4-in., and I found the closer I was gettin' the better I was hittin'. We put her down at 7:15, almost in the dark. It was a devilish good scrap."

After this performance, it was not surprising to find his

name among the list of C.B.'s [Knights Commander of the Bath].

A word of praise must be given to the resistance offered by the German squadron, who, outmatched both in weight and guns and numbers, fought a very gallant action until their ships sank beneath, their colours flying.

—*Falklands, Jutland and the Bight,*
by Commander the Hon. Barry Bingham,
V.C., R.N., John Murray Ltd., London, 1919

♦♦♦ *The Falklands was a most unbalanced victory. The Germans lost 2,300 men along with four warships and two colliers. Only the* Dresden *effected a temporary escape. Admiral von Spee, who was not among the survivors, had expressed a premonition when he was ashore in Valparaiso following the slaughter of Cradock's squadron. He had declined a spray of flowers a German woman had thrust at him, with the gloomy admonition, "Keep them for my funeral."*

The Royal Navy's price for the Falklands was ten killed, fifteen wounded.

Never again did the Kaiser hazard an entire squadron so far from home waters. Nor, for that matter, did Adolf Hitler in a subsequent conflict.

The Kent's *captain, John D. Allen, later wrote that he ceased firing when he realized* Nürnberg *was helpless and "burning gloriously." He added, "At 7:26 she heeled right over on her starboard side, lay there for a few seconds, then slowly turned over and quietly disappeared under the water.*

Just before she turned over we saw a group of men on her quarterdeck waving a German ensign attached to a staff . . . the sea was covered with bits of wreckage, oars, hammocks, chairs and a considerable number of men were holding on to them or swimming in the sea. It was a ghastly sight. There was so little we could do about it . . . only 12 men were picked up altogether, and out of these only seven survived." ◆◆◆

Jutland—a Clash of Dinosaurs

◆◆◆ *On Wednesday, May 31, 1916, and into the early hours of Thursday, the largest and deadliest naval engagement in history was fought in the North Sea. "Jutland" the battle became known among the Allies, the "Skaggerak" fight to the Germans and the Central Powers. It took place one hundred miles off Horns Reef and the Danish coast, with the participants 149 British ships and 116 German, ranging from 30,000-ton monster battle cruisers down to tiny torpedo boats.*

The cast of 100,000 officers and men was led by Admiral Sir John Jellicoe, commanding the Grand Fleet, and Admiral Reinhard Scheer, leader of the High Seas Fleet, the pride of Kaiser Wilhelm II. The gunnery of the German fleet had been the envy of the world's other navies several years before the beginning of the European War, as World War I was then best known.

Thus far, the war at sea could have best been described by one adjective: "inconclusive." The dramatic raiding by the Emden *and the equally spectacular elimination of von*

Spee's squadron were not in themselves actions capable of producing the ultimate victory or defeat for either combatant. True, the U-boat campaign was sinking more and more Allied merchant ships, but at the same time Imperial Germany's resources, especially manpower, were dwindling at a rate that soon would become alarming.

For the nearly two years of the war, there had been a growing demand in Great Britain, who possessed the largest fleet in the world, for a showdown fight with her opponent. Scheer had obviously based his entire strategy on the avoidance of just such a battle to the finish. His warships swept out of their anchorage at Wilhelmshaven only for hit-and-run raids, sometimes against the East Anglia coast, and then raced back for sanctuary.

Jutland took place only because Scheer and his scrappier battle-cruiser chief, Franz von Hipper, had sought, once again, to pick away at a small portion of the Royal Navy. This time, almost all of the Grand Fleet was already in the North Sea and prepared for battle.

Admiral Sir David Beatty, himself a most aggressive officer, led his battle cruisers into the opening phases of the massive action.

The following account of the duel to the death in the furrowed waters off of Horns Reef is by a lieutenant in the Royal Naval Reserve. Stephen King-Hall followed the family's nautical tradition. An uncle, Admiral Herbert King-Hall, was commander of the Cape of Good Hope Squadron. His father was the retired Admiral Sir George King-Hall.

Twenty-three years old and just out of training at Dartmouth Naval College, King-Hall served in H.M.S. South-

hampton *under Commander William E. E. Goodenough, who also flew the flag of the commander of the Second Light Cruiser Squadron. The* Southampton, *launched in 1912, was listed at 5,400 tons, mounted a main battery of eight 6-inch guns, and possessed a top speed of twenty-five knots.*

This is his view of the fantastic encounter: ◆◆◆

As the battle cruisers turned into line, I caught a faint distant glimpse of the silvery hulls of the German battle cruisers, though owing to the great range only parts of their upper works were visible for short intervals. They appeared to be steering a slightly converging course.

As the battle cruisers came into line, with the *Champion,* her destroyers and ourselves ahead of them, both our own battle cruisers and the Germans opened fire practically simultaneously.

Our line consisted of the *Lion, Princess Royal, Queen Mary, Tiger, New Zealand,* and *Indefatigable* in the order named.

The Germans were almost entirely merged into a long, smoky cloud on the eastern horizon, the sort of cloud that presages a thunderstorm, and from this gloomy retreat a series of red flashes darting out in our direction indicated the presence of five German battle cruisers.

It was at once evident that though the Germans were but indifferently visible to us, we on the other hand were silhouetted against a bright and clear western horizon, as far as the enemy were concerned. The German shooting, as has been the case throughout the war, was initially of an excellent quality. Our battle cruisers about a mile away just on our port quarter were moving along in a forest of tremendous splashes. Their guns trained over on the port beam were firing regular salvos.

At 4:15 I was watching our line from my position in the after control, when without any warning an immense column of grey smoke with a fiery base and a flaming top stood up on the sea, where the [18,750-ton] *Indefatigable* should have been. It hung there for I don't know how many seconds, and then a hole appeared in this pillar of smoke, through which I caught a glimpse of the forepart of the *Indefatigable* lying on its side; then there was a streak of flame and a fresh outpouring of smoke.

I turned with a sinking heart and watched the remaining five battle cruisers. I can—nor could I next day—remember no noise. We were not, of course, firing ourselves, and it seemed to me that I was being carried along in a kind of dream.

I wondered what would happen next; each time the splashes rose on either side of the line of great ships it was like a blow to the body. We could not see from our low deck where the 13.5-inch shells were falling on that sinister eastern horizon from which the maddening jets of flame darted in and out.

At 4:23, in the flicker of an eyelid, the beautiful [30,000-ton] *Queen Mary* was no more. A huge stem of grey smoke shot up to perhaps a thousand feet, swaying slightly at the base. The top of this stem of smoke expanded and rolled downwards. Flames rose and fell. in the stalk of this monstrous mushroom.

[Both the *Queen Mary* and the *Indefatigable* had gone,

as a German observer gasped, "like powder casks!" Admiral Beatty, who thought so, too, turned to his flag captain, to utter a classic understatement, "There seems to be something wrong with our bloody ships, today."]

The bows of a ship, a bridge, a mast, slid out of the smoke —perhaps after all the *Queen Mary* was still there.

No! it was the next astern—the *Tiger*.

Incredible as it may sound, the *Tiger* passed right over the spot on which the *Queen Mary* had been destroyed, and felt nothing. The time interval between her passage over the grave of the *Queen Mary* and the destruction of the latter ship would be about 40–60 seconds.

Just before the *Tiger* appeared, I saw some piece of debris go whirling up a full 1,000 feet above the top of the smoke—it might have been the armour plates from the top of a turret. I remember that I found it impossible to realize that I had just seen 2,000 men, and many personal friends, killed; it seemed more like a wonderful cinematograph picture.

What did worry me was that we were now reduced to four. I remember saying, "At this rate, by 5 P.M. we shall have no battle cruisers. But, by the laws of chance one of them will blow up next, you see."

We were by now right ahead of the *Lion* [Beatty's 30,000-ton battle cruiser flagship] and as I watched her, I saw a tremendous flash amidships, as she was hit by a shell or shells. I saw the whole ship stagger; for what seemed eternity I held my breath, half expecting her to blow up, but she held on and showed no signs of outward injury.

Actually her midship turret, manned by the Marines, was

completely put out of action, and had it not been for the heroism of the major of Marines [Major F. J. W. Harvey who, mortally wounded, ordered the magazines flooded], the ship might have gone. He lost his life and gained the V.C.

Soon after the *Lion* received this blow the Thirteenth Flotilla was ordered to make an attack on the German line. It was extremely difficult to see the destroyers after they started, but I could vaguely see that they were coming under heavy fire as they got about half-way across.

It was during this attack that *Nestor* and *Nomad* were lost and Commander Bingham gained his Victoria Cross.

At 4:38 a very startling development took place. From the *Southampton* we suddenly saw and reported light cruisers followed by the High Seas Fleet bearing Southeast. Sir David Beatty at once signalled to the battle cruiser force to alter course 16 points [180 degrees]. This maneuver was executed by the battle cruisers in succession.

[Beatty's basic strategy had been a dual one—keeping the battle joined and endeavoring to place his fleet between the enemy and his home ports. These tactics would have been heartily applauded by Nelson, John Paul Jones, or any of the sea's immortal warriors. Now, however, he had, inflexibly and with great daring, altered his plans in order to lead the German battleships toward Admiral Jellicoe's approaching main fleet.]

We disobeyed the signal, or rather delayed obeying it for two reasons—

Firstly, we wished to get close enough to the High Seas Fleet to examine them and report accurately on their composition and disposition. Secondly, we had hopes of delivering a torpedo attack on the long crescent-shaped line of heavy ships which were stretched round on our port bow.

It was a strain steaming at 25 knots straight for this formidable line of battleships, with our own friends going fast away from us in the opposite direction. As we got closer I counted sixteen or seventeen battleships with the four *König* class in the van and the six older pre-dreadnoughts in the rear.

Seconds became minutes and still they did not open fire, though every second I expected to see a sheet of flame ripple down their sides and a hail of shell fall around us. I can only account for this strange inactivity on their part by the theory that as they only saw us end on, and we were steering on opposite courses to the remaining British ships, they assumed we were a German light cruiser squadron that had been running away from the British battle cruisers.

Only in this manner can I account for the strange fact that they allowed us to get to within 13,000 yards of their line, and never fired a shot at us. This theory is supported by the fact that when at 4:45 the calm voice of Petty Officer Barnes on the foremost rangefinder intoned, "Range one, three, five, double ho! Range one, three, two, double ho!" The commodore saw that we could not get into a position for a torpedo attack, and as we should be lucky if we got out of the place we were then in, he gave the order for the turning signal, which had been flying for five minutes, to be hauled down.

Over went the helms, and the four ships slewed round,

bringing our sterns to the enemy. As we turned, the fun began, and half a dozen German battleships opened a deliberate fire on the squadron.

My action station was aft, but I could hear everything that passed on the fore-bridge, as I was in direct communication by voice-pipe. I heard the imperturbable Petty Officer Barnes, continuing his range taking—"Range one, three, two, double ho! Range one, double three, double ho!"

Crash! Bang! Whizzzz! and a salvo crumped down around us, the fragments whistling and sobbing overhead. Suddenly I heard Petty Officer Barnes say, with evident satisfaction, "Range obscured!"

About three or four miles north of us our battle cruisers were steaming along making a good deal of smoke and firing steadily, at what I imagined to be the German battle cruisers' distant hulls on our starboard bow.

Then came a gap of two miles, between the battle cruisers and the Fifth Battle Squadron.

These latter four ships had passed the battle cruisers on opposite courses when Sir David Beatty turned north, and as soon as they had passed him, Rear-Admiral H. Evan Thomas had turned his [Fifth Battle] squadron to north by west, and followed up the battle cruisers.

It will be remembered that whilst this was going on we [Second Light Cruiser Squadron] had still been going south. When we turned to north, we found ourselves about a mile behind the last ship of the Fifth Battle Squadron. Our squadron was not in line, but scattered.

As flagship we had the post of honor nearest to the

enemy. We maintained this position for one hour, during which time we were under persistent shell-fire from the rear six ships of the German line.

But we had them under observation, and we were able to transmit news of great importance to Sir John Jellicoe, whom we knew to be hurrying down from the north to our support. We had experienced one shock to the system, on sighting the German Fleet right ahead, and we all anticipated that the Huns would shortly enjoy the same sensation.

The Fifth Battle Squadron just ahead of us were a brave sight. They were receiving the concentrated fire of some twelve German heavy ships, but it did not seem to be worrying them, and though I saw several shells hit the *Warspite* just ahead of us, the German shooting at these ships did not impress me very favourably. Our own position was not pleasant.

The half-dozen older battleships at the tail of the German line were out of range to fire at the Fifth Battle Cruiser, but though we had gradually drawn out to 15,000–16,000 yards, we were inside their range, and they began to do a sort of target practice in slow time on our squadron.

I was in the after control with half a dozen men. We crouched down behind the tenth of an inch plating and ate bully beef, but it didn't seem to go down very easily. It seemed rather a waste of time to eat beef, for surely in the next ten minutes one of those 11-inch shells would get us, they couldn't go on falling just short and just over indefinitely, and, well, if one did hit us—light cruisers were not designed to digest 11-inch high explosives in their stomachs.

We could never resist having a peep about once a minute,

and somehow we always seemed to look just as two or three of the great brutes flickered flames from their guns at us, and we knew that another salvo was on its way across . . . the time of flight was twenty-three seconds.

Frequently they were so close that torrents of spray from the splashes splattered down on the boat deck. Each shell left a muddy pool in the water, and appeared to burst on impact.

We all compared notes afterwards and decided that during this hour about fifty to sixty shells fell within 100 yards of the ship, and many more slightly farther off. I attribute our escape, as far as we were able to contribute towards it, to the very clever manner in which our navigator zig-zagged the ship according to where he estimated the next salvo would fall. It was possible to forecast this to a certain extent, as it was obvious that the Huns were working what is technically known as "a ladder."

That is to say, the guns are fired with an increase of range to each salvo until "the target is crossed," and then the range is decreased for each salvo until the splashes are short of the target once again. It is thus a creeping barrage which moves up and down across the target.

The best way to avoid it, is to sheer in towards the enemy when the groups of tall splashes are coming towards the ship, and as soon as they have crossed over and begin once more to come towards the ship, then reverse the helm and sheer away from the enemy.

The fascination of watching these deadly and graceful splashes rising mysteriously from the smooth sea was enormous. To know that the next place where they would rise was being calculated by some Hun perched up in one of these distant masts, and that he was watching those "leetle cruiser ships" through a pair of Zeiss binoculars—and I was watching his ship through a similar pair of Zeiss—was really very interesting. It would have been very interesting indeed if I could have been calculating the position of the splashes round his ship; but he was 16,000 yards away, and our gunsights stopped at 14,500, so we just had to sit and hope we'd see the Grand Fleet soon.

At 6:17 P.M. the news that the Grand Fleet had been sighted right ahead spread around the ship like wild-fire. Forgotten was the steady shelling—now we'd give them hell. The battle drew on to its dramatic climax when as faintly ahead in the smoke and haze the great line of Grand Fleet battleships became visible curling across to the eastward.

They had just deployed.

Then two armoured cruisers appeared from right ahead between ourselves and the German line. They were steering about south-west, and were moving in an appalling concentration of fire from the German battleships.

Who could they be?

As I watched, the leading ship glowed red all over and seemed to burst in every direction. Our men cheered frantically, thinking it was a German. Alas! I had caught a brief glimpse of a white ensign high above the smoke and flame. It was the 14,000-ton *Defence* flying the flag of the gallant Sir Robert Arbuthnot.

The ship astern was the [old, 13,500-ton cruiser] *Warrior,* and it was evident that she was hard hit.

The Huns redoubled their efforts upon her, when a most extraordinary incident amazed both sides. The [battle cruiser] *Warspite,* just ahead of us, altered course to starboard and proceeded straight for the centre of the Hun line. For some moments she was unfired at, then as she continued to go straight for the Germans the tornado of fire lifted from the *Warrior,* hovered as it seemed in space, and fell with a crash about the *Warspite.*

The *Warrior,* burning in several places, battered and wrecked, with steam escaping from many broken pipes, dragged slowly out of the battle to the westward; she passed about 400 yards under our stern.

Meanwhile, with sinking heart, I watched the *Warspite* and wondered what her amazing career portended. I focused her in my reflex camera, but so certain did I feel that she would be destroyed that I could not bring myself to expose the plate. I should guess that she reached a position about 8,000 yards from the German line when to our relief she slowly turned round, and still lashing out viciously with all her 15-inch guns she rejoined the British lines. At our end of the line there was a distinct lull. In fact, the speed of the tail of the Fleet became so slow that our squadron turned 32 points [a complete circle] in order not to bunch up on the battleships. In the course of this maneuver we very nearly had a collision with one of the Fifth Battle Squadron, the *Valiant* or *Malaya* . . .

Far ahead, rapid flashes and much smoke indicated that furious attacks and counterattacks were taking place between the rival destroyer flotillas and their supporting light cruisers. The battle area of these desperate conflicts between gun platforms of ¼-inch steel, moving at the speed of an express train, was the space between the vans of the two fleets.

We were too far off to see any details of this fighting; but at 6:47 we reached the spot where it had taken place. The first thing we saw was a German three-funnel cruiser, the *Wiesbaden.* She was battered badly, as she had been lying inert between the two lines, and whenever a British battleship could not see her target she opened on the *Wiesbaden.*

We were simply longing to hit something, and this seemed our chance. Increasing speed to 20 knots we turned and led our squadron in to administer the *coup de grace.* Turning to bring our broadsides to bear at 6,000 yards, we directed a stream of 6-inch on the Hun, who replied feebly with one gun. There is no doubt that the men who worked that gun had the right spirit in them.

Beyond the *Wiesbaden,* at a range of about 14,000 yards, our old friends, the pre-dreadnoughts were toddling along at the stern of the German line. During our approach to the *Wiesbaden* they had preserved an ominous silence. It did not remain thus for long. The six of them opened a rapid fire on us, and we were at once obliged to open the range without delay.

We scuttled back to the tail of the British line as hard as we could, zig-zagging like snipe with 11-inch crumping down ahead, on both sides, and astern of us.

I counted a bunch of three about 40 yards on the starboard beam of the ship, and an officer who was hanging out over the other side of the after control, reported a group of seven close to the ship on the port beam. At this period twilight was beginning, and the visibility was partly spoiled by low-lying clouds of funnel and brown cordite smoke, which hung like a gloomy pall over the scene.

It was apparent from the curve of our line that we were gradually working round to the eastward of the Huns, and at 7:30 P.M. the Germans decided to make a supreme effort to get out of the nasty position they were being forced into, viz., the centre of a semicircle, of which the British Fleet was the circumference.

That they got out very cleverly must be admitted. A few destroyers crept out at the head of their line, and almost immediately afterwards a dense smokescreen unfurled itself between us and the enemy. Before this screen had reached its full length the Germans were altering course 8 points together to starboard, and escaping from the deadly fire of the British battleships.

One of the minor incidents of battle now took place.

A German destroyer, part of the debris of the destroyer actions some twenty minutes earlier, was lying, incapable of movement, between the two fleets. Unfortunately for her, she was in such a position that the smokescreen rolled to the southward of her. She was alone for her sins in front of the British Fleet.

No battleship fired at her; but we gave her a salvo at 6,000 yards as we came abreast of her. We hit, and a large explosion took place amidships. However, she still managed to float, and the *Faulkner* and some destroyers, who were hanging about near us, went over and finished her off. It rather annoyed us, as we intended to do some more target practice on her.

The Germans had disappeared somewhere to the southwest behind their smoke, and for a few minutes everything was strangely calm.

At 8:25 the *Birmingham* sighted a submarine, and I saw that the Grand Fleet had got into five columns for the night. Four columns were abreast of each other, and the fifth, composed of the *Valiant, Malaya,* and *Barham* [Evan-Thomas' flagship], was astern of them. We were on the starboard beam of this latter column. The course of the Fleet was south, and the Germans were somewhere to the westward of us in the growing darkness.

At 8:50 P.M. we sighted four German destroyers approaching us on the starboard bow, apparently intending to deliver an attack on the Fifth Battle Squadron. We opened fire at once, and hit the leading destroyer amidships. All four turned round and, pursued by our shells, disappeared behind a smokescreen . . .

At about 10 P.M. searchlights criss-crossed on the western horizon; they rose and fell, turned and twisted, and finally fixed their implacable and relentless light on a group of destroyers. Fascinated, we watched the destroyers rushing up the bright paths of the lights. The white splashes gleamed all round them, and then a great red lurid stain started in one of the attacking craft and spread to a vast explosion of fierce white flame, beside which the cruel searchlights seemed pale. Instantly the searchlights were extinguished, the attack was over, and once more all was dark.

We had probably witnessed one of the many and glorious attacks in which the British destroyer flotillas threw themselves without stint upon the German Fleet throughout this strange night.

The sudden disappearing of all signs of this attack ever having been made, left a curious feeling of emptiness in the atmosphere. I groped my way on to the bridge and had a chat with the gunnery lieutenant, as a result of which he arranged that in the event of night action he would control the guns from the fore-bridge and I would be in general charge aft.

A signalman, Ireland, and the navigator suddenly whispered, "Five ships on the beam!"

The Commodore looked at them through night glasses, and I heard a whispered discussion going on as to whether they were the enemy or the Third Light Cruiser Squadron.

From their faint silhouettes it was impossible to discover more than the fact that they were light cruisers. I decided to go aft as quickly as possible.

On the way aft I looked in at the after control, where I was advised, "There are five Huns on the beam. What on earth is going on?"

They were evidently in as much doubt as us, for as I got down into the waist by the mainmast, a very great many things happened in a very short time. We began to challenge; the Germans switched on coloured lights at their fore yardarms.

A second later a solitary gun crashed forth from the *Dublin,* who was next astern of us. Simultaneously I saw the shell hit a ship just above the water-line and about 800 yards away.

As I caught a nightmare-like glimpse of her interior, which has remained photographed on my mind to this day, I said to myself: "My God, they are alongside us!"

At that moment the Germans switched on their search-lights, and we switched on ours. Before I was blinded by the lights in my eyes I caught sight of a line of light grey ships. Then the gun behind which I was standing answered my shout of "Fire!"

The action lasted 3½ minutes. The four leading German ships concentrated their lights and guns on the *Southampton;* the fifth and perhaps the fourth as well fired at the *Dublin*. The *Nottingham* and *Birmingham,* third and fourth in our line, with great wisdom did not switch on their lights and were not fired at.

In those 3½ minutes we had 89 casualties, and 75 per cent of the personnel on the upper deck were killed or wounded. It is impossible to give a connected account of what happened. Many strange and unpleasant things happen when men find themselves in hell on earth. Men—strong men—go mad and jump overboard. Wounded men are driven to the oblivion of death in the sea by the agony of their injuries. It is not good to look too closely into these things which are the realities, the plain facts of battle.

The range was amazingly close—no two groups of such ships have ever fought so close in the history of this war. There could be no missing. A gun was fired and a hit obtained—the gun was loaded, it flamed, it roared, it leapt to the rear, it slid to the front—there was another hit.

The range was so close, the German shots went high, just high enough to burst on the upper deck and around the after superstructure and bridge. One shell had burst on the side just below the gun, and the fragments had whipped over the top of the low bulwark and mowed the men down as standing corn falls before the reaper. Another shell had burst on the searchlight just above us, and hurled the remains of this expensive instrument many feet. Three men who looked after it and had guided its beam onto the enemy died instantaneously.

The fragments from this shell descended upon the waist like hail, and scoured out the insides of the gun-shields of the two 6-inch, manned by marines, one gun each side. And then I seemed to be standing in a fire. The flash of some exploding shell had ignited half a dozen rounds of cordite.

A shell exploding in the half-deck had severed the connection to the upper deck fire main. I put my head down a hatch and shouted for a good hose. The wine steward came up on deck with one, someone turned on the water down below, and the fire was quickly out.

The wine steward forgot his servitude, he rose to the heights of an officer, he was my right-hand man. He spoke words of fierce exhortation to the wounded; those who could get up did so.

Then it became lighter than the day. I looked forward. Two pillars of white flame rose splendidly aloft. One roared up the foremast, the other reached above the tops of the second and third funnels.

Where were the Germans? Nothing but groans from dark corners. Though I did not know it at the time, the Germans had fled because our torpedo lieutenant had fired a 21-inch torpedo. At 41 knots the torpedo had shot across and, striking the [light cruiser] *Frauenlob,* had blown her in half. Out of nearly 350 in her, 7 survived.

I have their account of the action before me.

They say, "The leading ship of the British line burst into flame and blew up . . . then we were torpedoed." They were wrong—their friends sheered off just a few seconds too soon.

I will admit that they probably think they saw us blown up. A friend of mine who was five miles away in one of the Fifth Battle Squadron, read a signal on the bridge by the light of our fires.

In the ships of our squadron astern they thought we had gone, and took shelter from the bits they expected to come down. It was a near thing . . .

We increased speed to 20 knots, and as dawn slowly grew the ghostly shapes of some battleships loomed out of the mist. I heard a pessimist on the upper bridge hazard the opinion that we were about to take station astern of the German Battle Fleet, but as the light grew brighter we saw that we had rejoined the British Fleet.

Complete daylight enabled us to survey the damage.

The funnels were riddled through with hundreds of small holes, and the decks were slashed and ripped with splinters. There were several holes along the side, but the general effect was as if handfuls of splinters had been thrown against the upper works of the ship. The protective mattresses round the bridge and control position were slashed with splinters. The foremast, the rigging, the boats, the signal lockers, the funnel casing, the main mast, everything was a mass of splinter holes.

Our sailors firmly believed, and continued to do so up to the day on which I left the ship, that we had been deluged with shrapnel. It was certainly surprising that anyone on the upper deck remained unhit.

The flag lieutenant had a remarkable escape. The secretary asked him what he had done to his cap during the night. He took it off, and there was a large rent where a splinter, which must have been shaped something like a skewer, had entered his cap just above his ear and out again through the crown.

> —*A Naval Lieutenant, 1914–'18,*
> by Stephen King-Hall, Methuen,
> London, 1919

♦♦♦ *The* Southampton, *forever to be known as the cruiser that destroyed the* Frauenlob, *limped back to port.*

Bingham, who had written of the Falklands from the decks of the Invincible, *had commanded the luckless destroyer* Nestor *at Jutland. He won the Victoria Cross—even if he lost his ship—in gallantly leading his flotilla in a torpedo attack against the German battle cruisers. The* Invincible, *belying her name, was also destroyed, with all but six out of one thousand aboard.*

More than six thousand Englishmen died, twice the number of their foe. Fourteen Royal Navy warships, aggregating 114,000 tons, were sunk, while eleven of the Kaiser's vessels, representing 63,015 tons were lost.

The aggressive Beatty soon assumed Jellicoe's command, and the latter became First Sea Lord.

Who really won at Jutland, where the huge steel dinosaurs of the seas met and clashed in quantity for the first—

and last—time? Naval strategists still debate the question. The fact remained—the High Seas Fleet never again offered battle. But neither did the Grand Fleet try to flush out her foe anew, any more than Jellicoe had attempted to pursue the badly hurt warships of the High Seas Fleet and deliver a coup de grace.

King-Hall became a well-known British author, playwright, and radio-television commentator. For a time he published a London newsletter, in which he warned against the dangers of a "nuclear balance of power." Knighted in 1954 and later made a baron, Lord King-Hall died in 1966. ◆◆◆

"I Think It Is a Pocket Battleship . . . !"

◆◆◆ *The framers of the Treaty of Versailles thought that, in allowing Germany to build 10,000-ton "pocket" battleships, they were ruling out future juggernauts similar to the ones that had accomplished such fearful execution at Jutland. But naval architects in Kiel and Hamburg, making the best of the limitations of the three authorized warships of this class, produced commerce raiders without peer.*

Although they were five or more knots slower than the vulnerable battle cruisers, the Deutschland, Admiral Scheer, *and* Admiral Graf Spee *could steam at twenty-five knots, were armored, and mounted a main battery of 11-inch guns. They could lob seaward a crushing broadside of nearly three tons.*

Under forty-five-year-old Captain Hans Langsdorff, who served at Jutland as a young officer, the Graf Spee *proved that she was indeed well tailored for her mission. In the three latter months of 1939, she sank nine British ships, representing more than fifty thousand tons, in the South Atlantic.*

To eliminate this overwhelming menace to sea commerce,

the Admiralty dispatched a modest cruiser division led by Commodore Henry Harwood Harwood, into southerly waters. Six years older than Langsdorff, "Bobby" Harwood, as fellow officers affectionately knew him, had served in the Grand Fleet aboard H.M.S. Royal Sovereign *and after the war on the staunch "unsinkable"* Southampton.

In late November, this unit—far weaker than the one Admiral Sturdee had been handed in 1914—consisted of H.M.S. Ajax *(7,000 tons) flying Harwood's broad pennant and commanded by Captain Charles H. L. Woodhouse, H.M.N.Z.S.* Achilles, *a sistership, under Captain W. Edward Parry, and H.M.S.* Exeter, *at 8,400 tons, the mightiest of the trio. The* Exeter, *under Captain F. S. Bell, offered a main battery of 8-inch guns, compared with the 6-inchers of her sisters.*

The combined broadsides of the three cruisers, however, was still 1,500 pounds lighter than that of the mighty Graf Spee. *Their ace was tremendous speed—a capacity for revving up to more than thirty-one knots in a relatively few minutes, assuming all boilers were fired.*

Their mission was to sweep the South Atlantic until they found and destroyed their formidable quarry. The following is the official Admiralty report of how Commodore Harwood led his squadron into the attack, off the coast of Uruguay and the mouth of the River Plate: ◆◆◆

On December 3rd, 1939, the three British cruisers were scattered over two thousand miles.

It was on the afternoon of that day that a report was received from the British S.S. *Doric Star* that she was being attacked by a German "pocket battleship" on the eastern side of the South Atlantic about midway between Sierra Leone and the Cape of Good Hope. The *Doric Star* had sent out the wireless message in spite of the fact that the German raider was firing on her in an attempt to prevent her from using her wireless.

Commodore Harwood correctly anticipated that the raider, knowing that she had been reported by the *Doric Star,* would leave that area and probably cross the South Atlantic. He estimated that the raider could reach the Rio de Janeiro area by the morning of December 12th, the River Plate area by that evening or the following morning, or the Falkland Islands area by December 14th.

There was nothing to indicate which of these three areas —separated from one another by more than 1,500 miles— was the raider's objective. Commodore Harwood decided, however, that the most important area to be defended was the focal area of the large and very valuable trade off the River Plate. He therefore ordered his squadron to concentrate 150 miles off the River Plate Estuary. He also made arrangements to ensure that his ships would not be short of fuel when they arrived at the rendezvous. All this was done in one short signal, after the transmission of which no wireless communication was used, since this would have indicated the movements of British forces to the enemy.

Accurate navigation led to the concentration of the British cruisers at the expected moment—7 A.M. on December 12th.

The greatest use was made of that day. Commodore Harwood explained to his captains the tactics which he proposed to use in the event of contact being made with the powerful raider. These tactics were then exercised by the squadron. It is noteworthy that the final words of Commodore Harwood's instructions to his captains were to act "without further orders so as to maintain decisive gun range."

Wednesday, December 13th, dawned fine and clear, with extreme visibility. There was a fairly strong breeze from the south-east, a low swell coming from the same quarter, and a slight sea. At 6:14 A.M. smoke was sighted on the horizon just abaft the port beam, and H.M.S. *Exeter* was ordered to investigate. Two minutes later *Exeter* reported, "I think it is a pocket battleship." The enemy was in sight. Contact had at last been made between British naval forces and the raider which they had been hunting for more than two months.

At the time of the sighting of the smoke, the *Admiral Graf Spee* and the British cruisers were steering converging courses. As soon as the smoke was identified as that of the German raider, the ships of the British squadron began to act in accordance with the tactics practised on the previous day. All ships increased speed and began to work up to full speed as rapidly as possible. The eight-inch gun cruiser, *Exeter,* the most powerful unit of the British squadron, made a large alteration course to the westward, while the two six-inch gun cruisers, *Ajax* and *Achilles,* forged ahead to the north-eastward, altering course slightly in order to close the range rapidly. These maneuvers were carried out so that the "pocket battleship" should be simultaneously engaged from widely different angles. This would force him either to "split" his main armament in order to engage both units, or to leave one of the British units unengaged by his eleven-inch guns.

At 6:18 A.M., only four minutes after the first sighting of smoke, the *Graf Spee* opened fire with her main armament of six eleven-inch guns. She had "split" her main armament, and one turret fired at H.M.S. *Exeter* and the other at *Ajax* and *Achilles*. The range was very long, but it was being shortened rapidly by all three of the British cruisers.

Two minutes later, at 6:20 A.M., *Exeter* opened fire with her two forward turrets—four eight-inch guns. The range was then 9½ sea miles. Her two after guns opened fire as soon as they would bear, two and a half minutes later. This eight-inch gunfire seemed to worry the enemy almost from the beginning. After shifting target rapidly once or twice, the *Graf Spee* concentrated the fire of all six of her eleven-inch guns on *Exeter*. The *Graf Spee*'s first salvo fell short of *Exeter*. The second was over, and the third straddled the cruiser.

Meanwhile *Ajax* and *Achilles* had opened fire with their six-inch guns. *Achilles* opened fire at 6:21 A.M. and *Ajax* two minutes later. These two six-inch gun cruisers immediately developed a high rate of fire, combined with great accuracy. The despatch of *Achilles* states that "fire appeared to become rapidly effective," while the despatch of *Ajax* states that "effective fire developed immediately."

At 6:23 A.M. an eleven-inch shell burst just short of *Exeter,* abreast the middle of the ship. Splinters from this shell killed the torpedo tubes crews, damaged the communications of the ship, and riddled the funnels and searchlights.

One minute later *Exeter* suffered a direct hit from an eleven-inch shell. This shell struck B turret, putting that turret and its two eight-inch guns out of action. Splinters from that shell swept the bridge. All the bridge personnel except the captain and two others were either killed or wounded. The wheelhouse communications were wrecked.

As soon as it was realized in the lower conning position that communications with the wheelhouse had ceased to function, that lower position took over the steering. Even so, the ship had begun to swing to starboard, and there was danger of the after guns becoming unable to bear on the target. This was noticed by the torpedo officer, who, on his own initiative, succeeded in getting an order through to the lower conning position which resulted in the ship being brought back to her course.

The captain of *Exeter* was at this time making his way aft. With the bridge out of action, he had decided to fight his ship from the after conning position. When he reached that position, however, he found that all communications from the after conning had been destroyed. The steering was therefore changed over to the after steering position, and communication established by means of a chain of messengers.

During this time *Exeter* received two more hits forward from eleven-inch shells, and also suffered some damage by splinters from shells bursting short.

Meanwhile *Ajax* and *Achilles* were making good and rapid shooting with their six-inch guns, and they were closing the range rapidly and drawing ahead on the enemy.

That this six-inch gunfire was causing the enemy trouble was shown by the fact that at 6:30 A.M. the *Graf Spee* again "split" her main armament, switching over one eleven-inch turret to engage the six-inch gun cruisers. This temporarily reduced the volume of heavy fire to which *Exeter* was subjected.

The secondary armament of the *Graf Spee*—5.9-inch guns—had been alternately engaging *Ajax* and *Achilles,* but without effect, although some salvoes had fallen close. These guns continued to fire at the six-inch gun cruisers.

At 6:32 A.M. *Exeter* fired her starboard torpedoes at the enemy. These torpedoes went wide, because the *Graf Spee,* apparently finding the British gunfire too hot, turned 150 degrees away under cover of a smoke screen before the torpedoes reached her. By 6:36 A.M. the six-inch gun cruisers were doing 28 knots. This rapid increase of speed—the ships had been doing 14 knots only 20 minutes previously— reflects great credit upon the engine and boiler room personnel.

At 6:37 A.M. *Ajax* catapulted her aircraft. As soon as the aircraft was in the air, it took up a position on the disengaged bow of the six-inch gun cruisers. At about 6:38 A.M. *Exeter* made a large alteration of course to starboard in order to bring her port torpedo tubes to bear on the enemy. As she was turning she received two more hits from eleven-inch shells. One of these hit the foremost turret, putting the turret and its two eight-inch guns out of action. The other entered the hull, did extensive damage and started a fierce fire between decks. The observer in *Ajax*'s aircraft reported that "she completely disappeared in smoke and flame and it was feared that she had gone. However, she emerged, and re-entered the action."

Exeter had, indeed, suffered severely from the much heavier metal of her adversary. Two of her three turrets were out of action, and the only two guns still in action were aft. All of her compass repeaters had been smashed, and the captain was conning the ship with the help of a small boat's compass. By this time *Exeter* had a seven degree list and was down by the bow, but was still steaming at full power.

At 6:40 A.M. an eleven-inch shell burst just short of *Achilles,* in line with the bridge. Splinters from this shell killed four ratings in the main gunnery control position and stunned the gunnery officer, as well as slightly wounding the captain and the chief yeoman of signals on the bridge. Fortunately these splinters did not put the director out of action or damage any important instrument. Nevertheless, the main control position was momentarily out of action through these casualties.

The secondary control position immediately took over the ship's armament, and continued the action until the main control was ready to resume some minutes later. The greatest gallantry and fortitude was shown by the surviving personnel. A sergeant of Royal Marines remained uncomplainingly at his post and carried out his duties until the end of the action although he was seriously wounded. A seaman boy behaved with exemplary coolness despite the carnage around him and continued his duty of passing information to the guns. He was at one time heard denying most vigorously a report of his own death which had spread round the ship. These were but two instances of gallantry in a fierce action memorable for the bearing of the personnel of the British cruisers.

After 6:40 A.M. the action became virtually a chase. The *Graf Spee* had turned away to the westward under cover of a smoke screen, and the two six-inch gun cruisers were hauling round to the north-westward in pursuit, accepting the fact that this entailed being unable to bring the after guns to bear on the enemy. They were by now doing 31 knots and still increasing speed.

At 7:16 A.M. the *Graf Spee* made a drastic alteration of course to port under cover of smoke. She was then steering almost directly for *Exeter,* and it seemed that her intention was to finish off that damaged cruiser. Four minutes later, however, the effective support of *Exeter*'s consorts obliged the *Graf Spee* to make another large alteration of course. She hauled round to the north-westward until all her eleven-inch guns would bear on *Ajax* and *Achilles,* and at once opened fire on the small British cruisers. The range at that time was 5½ miles. *Ajax* was straddled by eleven-inch salvoes, but she was not hit.

At 7:25 A.M. *Ajax* was hit by an eleven-inch shell. This shell put X turret out of action, and, by a stroke of bad luck, it also led to the jamming of Y turret. Thus this one shell robbed *Ajax* of the use of four of her guns, besides causing a number of casualties.

It was at about this time that the pilot of *Ajax*'s aircraft, which had been spotting the fall of shot for the six-inch gun cruisers, decided to approach the *Graf Spee* in an attempt to discover the extent of damage that ship had received. As soon as the aircraft came within range of the enemy's anti-aircraft guns, these opened fire. As the primary and most important duty of the aircraft was spotting the fall of shot for the control of the British cruisers' gunfire, the aircraft retired out of range of the enemy's anti-aircraft guns.

Exeter had been dropping gradually astern, as she had been forced to reduce speed owing to the damage forward. She still continued in action, however, engaging the enemy with her two remaining guns firing in local control under the direction of an officer standing in an exposed position on the searchlight platform. At about 7:30 A.M., however, *Exeter*'s remaining turret ceased to operate due to flooding. Thus, *Exeter* could no longer engage the enemy nor keep up with the action. Reluctantly, therefore, she was forced to break off the action, and at about 7:40 A.M. she turned to the south-east and steamed away at slow speed, starting to repair damage and make herself seaworthy.

At 7:28 A.M. *Ajax* and *Achilles* hauled round to a westerly course in order to close the range still further. Three minutes later *Ajax*'s aircraft reported, "Torpedoes approaching. They will pass ahead of you." Commodore Harwood, however, decided to take no chances, and the cruisers made a large alteration of course towards the enemy in order to avoid the torpedoes. This alteration of course had the effect of closing the range very rapidly. At this time *Ajax* had only three guns in action, as an accident prevented one gun of B turret from being fired, while both X and Y turrets were out of action as a result of the eleven-inch shell hit sustained at 7:25 A.M. Nevertheless, the enemy did not relish the fire of the small British cruisers. The *Graf*

Spee turned away to the westward almost immediately, making much smoke and zig-zagging in an attempt to throw out the British gunfire.

At this stage of the action the shooting of the six-inch gun cruisers appeared very accurate. *Achilles* was making excellent practice with her eight guns, while *Ajax* was making very good use of her three remaining guns. At 7:36 A.M. the *Graf Spee* turned to the south-westward in order to bring all her heavy guns to bear on the British cruisers in an attempt to fight them off. The two small British cruisers stood on, however, and by 7:38 A.M. the range was down to 4 miles.

It was then reported that so many rounds had been expended during the continuous periods of rapid firing that there was some danger of running short of ammunition, if the action was prolonged without reaching a decision. This led Commodore Harwood to adopt an immediate change in tactics. He considered that by breaking off the day action and shadowing the enemy till nightfall, he would have a better chance of closing to a range at which his lighter armament and torpedoes would have a decisive effect.

Accordingly, at 7:40 A.M., Commodore Harwood turned *Ajax* and *Achilles* away to the eastward under cover of a smoke screen. Just as the ships began to turn, an eleven-inch shell from one of the *Graf Spee*'s last salvoes brought down the main topmast of *Ajax*. The bursting of this shell caused some casualties, and the falling of the mast destroyed the wireless aerials. Spare aerials were, however, soon rigged.

The *Graf Spee* made no attempt to follow the British cruisers, but continued to steam to the westward at a speed of about 22 knots.

After opening the range by steaming to the eastward under cover of a smoke screen for six minutes, Commodore Harwood again turned his ships to the westward and ordered them to take up positions for shadowing the enemy.

At 8:07 A.M., and every hour thereafter, the British cruisers broadcast the position, course, and speed of the German raider, so that British merchant ships in the vicinity would keep out of danger.

Just before 9:15 A.M. *Ajax* recovered her aircraft. The conditions were difficult, but the operation was carried out with great skill and—what was so important—without loss of time.

Commodore Harwood's objective remained the destruction of the enemy in close action after nightfall, but he had to take steps to deal with the situation which might arise if the *Graf Spee* succeeded in eluding night action. He could not risk further prolonged day action with his superior adversary owing to the weakening of his force by the departure of *Exeter* and the quantity of ammunition remaining in his six-inch gun cruisers. It was necessary, therefore, to secure reinforcements so that nothing should be left to chance.

The nearest British warship was the 10,000 ton eight-inch gun cruiser *Cumberland*, at the Falkland Islands. At 9:46 A.M. Commodore Harwood ordered her to proceed to the River Plate area at full speed. H.M.S. *Cumberland* had, however, picked up jumbled messages which indicated that an action was in progress to the northward, and she had already left the Falkland Islands on the initiative of her commanding officer before these orders were received. On receipt of Commodore Harwood's signal *Cumberland* increased to full speed.

Meanwhile, other operations were set on foot by the Admiralty. Orders were given for the aircraft carrier H.M.S. *Ark Royal* and the battlecruiser H.M.S. *Renown,* and other ships all of which had been operating some 3,000 miles away, to proceed at once to the South American coast, and steps were taken to ensure that adequate supplies of fuel would be available at various strategic points.

By 10:05 A.M. *Achilles,* who had over-estimated the speed of the *Graf Spee,* had closed the range to eleven and a half miles. The *Graf Spee* then altered course and fired two three-gun salvoes of eleven-inch at *Achilles.* The fact that the *Graf Spee* altered course sufficiently to bring her forward turret to bear in order to fire these salvoes suggests that the enemy's after eleven-inch turret was out of action at that time. The first of these salvoes from the *Graf Spee* fell very short, but the second fell close to *Achilles,* which ship was already under helm. *Achilles* turned away at full speed under cover of a smoke screen and resumed shadowing from a longer range.

An hour later a merchant ship was sighted fairly close to the *Graf Spee.* She appeared to be stopped and blowing off steam. A few minutes later *Ajax* and *Achilles* received a signal from the *Graf Spee.* It read: "*Ajax* and *Achilles* from *Graf Spee.* Please pick up lifeboats of English steamer."

On coming up with the merchant ship H.M.S. *Ajax* found that she was the British S.S. *Shakespeare,* and that all her boats were hoisted. *Ajax* signalled to her asking if she required assistance, and the *Shakespeare* replied that she was quite all right and did not require assistance. It would appear, therefore, that the signal of the *Graf Spee* to *Ajax* was a ruse adopted by the German raider in an attempt to shake off her tenacious pursuers.

The shadowing of the *Graf Spee* by *Ajax* and *Achilles* continued without further incident until 7:15 P.M. At this time the *Graf Spee* altered course and re-opened fire on *Ajax* with her eleven-inch guns at a range of thirteen miles. *Ajax* at once turned away under cover of a smoke screen and resumed a shadowing position out of range.

By this time it was clear that the *Graf Spee* intended to enter the estuary of the River Plate. The entrance to the River Plate Estuary is guarded by a sandbank sixteen miles long, running across the estuary. This is known as English Bank. Commodore Harwood considered that the *Graf Spee* might try to elude the British cruisers and break back to the open sea by doubling round this sandbank. He therefore disposed his forces so as to prevent the enemy slipping out. As soon as the *Graf Spee* passed the Island of Lobos, and was therefore committed to entering the estuary of the River Plate, the whole duty of shadowing the enemy devolved upon *Achilles,* while *Ajax* proceeded to the south of English Bank so that she would meet the *Graf Spee* if she tried to double back towards the open sea after rounding the sandbank.

The sun set at 8:48 P.M. and the *Graf Spee* was, from *Achilles,* clearly silhouetted at a range of about twelve and a half miles. *Achilles* altered course to the north-westward in order to take full advantage of the afterglow. She had already increased speed in order to close the enemy before dark.

By 10:02 P.M. *Achilles* had closed to five miles from the *Graf Spee,* and it was possible to determine that the enemy was heading to pass to the northward of English Bank. *Achilles* informed *Ajax* accordingly.

Soon after that time *Achilles* found the *Graf Spee* very difficult to see owing to low clouds and patches of smoke. The British cruiser accordingly hauled to the southward in order to get the enemy silhouetted against the lights of Montevideo. This maneuver was successful.

At 10:48 the *Graf Spee* was observed to be about seven miles east of the whistle buoy at the entrance to the Montevideo channel, and it was clear that the defeated German raider was about to seek the shelter of the neutral harbour of Montevideo. The *Graf Spee* anchored in Montevideo roads at ten minutes past midnight.

Commodore Harwood had called off the pursuit an hour before the *Graf Spee* anchored, since the enemy's intentions had been by that time clear, and the British commander was at pains to respect neutral territorial waters.

[There was now time for both sides to count the casualties: 72 killed in the British squadron, most of them on the *Exeter,* and 23 wounded, while 37 died and 58 were wounded aboard the *Graf Spee.* Most of the pocket battleship dead were buried in solemn ceremonies ashore, in the presence of large numbers of the German colony in Uruguay.]

At 10 P.M. on that day—Thursday, 14th December—

the cruiser *Cumberland* arrived in the River Plate area, having made the long passage from the Falkland Islands in thirty-four hours. This reinforcement enabled Commodore Harwood to dispose his forces so that sectors to seaward of all three of the deep-water channels leading out of the River Plate Estuary could be watched during the night. *Cumberland* patrolled the centre sector, with *Achilles* to the north of her and *Ajax* to the southward. Should the *Graf Spee* come out, she was to be shadowed, and the three British cruisers were to concentrate sufficiently far to seaward to enable a concerted attack to be delivered on the enemy.

Next day—Friday, 15th December—another problem faced Commodore Harwood. His ships could not keep the sea indefinitely, with boilers always ready to drive the ships at full speed, without further supplies of fuel. The Royal Fleet Auxiliary tanker *Olynthus* was in the vicinity, and *Ajax* was ordered to oil from her at sea, while the operation was covered by the other two cruisers. Fuelling at sea is a difficult operation in anything but a flat calm, and it was by no means calm. Securing wires, and even two spans of hurricane hawsers, were parted, but the fuelling was successfully accomplished.

Shortly after this, Commodore Harwood received news that the *Graf Spee* had been granted an extension of her stay in Montevideo up to seventy-two hours, in order to make herself seaworthy. Nevertheless, Harwood's despatch states: "I could feel no security that she would not break out at any moment." The strain of watching and waiting, in instant readiness for action, could in no way be relaxed.

About 5:30 P.M. on the afternoon of Sunday, December

17th, news was received by Harwood stating that the *Graf Spee* was weighing anchor.

Cumberland, Ajax and *Achilles* at once altered course towards the entrance of the five-mile dredged channel leading into Montevideo roads and the crews went to action stations. *Ajax*'s aircraft was flown off, with orders to report the position and movements of the *Graf Spee* and of the German ship *Tacoma,* to which ship the *Graf Spee* was known to have transferred a large number of men.

The *Graf Spee* left harbour at 6:15 P.M. and proceeded slowly down the dredged channel, after leaving the end of which she turned to the westward. The *Tacoma* also weighed anchor and followed the *Graf Spee.*

Ajax's aircraft reported the *Graf Spee* in a position in shallow water about six miles south-west of Montevideo, and shortly afterwards—at 8:54 P.M.—the aircraft signalled, "*Graf Spee* has blown herself up."

The British cruisers carried on towards Montevideo, proceeding north of the English Bank. *Ajax* recovered her aircraft, and as she was doing so, *Achilles* passed her. The two cruisers which had done such excellent service cheered ship as they passed one another.

Navigation lights were switched on, and the British squadron steamed past the whistle buoy at the entrance to the Montevideo dredged channel, passing within about four miles of the wreck of the *Graf Spee*. Harwood's despatch stated: "It was now dark, and she was ablaze from end to end, flames reaching almost as high as the top of the control tower, a magnificent and most cheering sight."

While *Cumberland, Ajax,* and *Achilles* were witnessing

the ignominious end of the ship which had been the pride of the German navy—which had represented Germany at the Coronation Review at Spithead, and which had carried Herr Hitler triumphantly to Memel—*Exeter,* who had contributed so gallantly to the *Graf Spee*'s defeat, was at the Falkland Islands.

—*The Battle of the River Plate,*
    The Admiralty, His Majesty's Stationery Office,
    London, 1940, reprinted by permission of the
    Controller of Her Britannic Majesty's Stationery Office

♦♦♦ *Langsdorff obviously had no idea of how badly he had hurt the British cruisers or how many thousands of miles distant further reinforcements actually were. He possibly could have made good the escape he had considered impossible. Two nights later, on December 19, brooding in his hotel room, he wrote a letter to the German Consul in Montevideo, concluding, "I shall meet my fate with firm faith in the cause and the future of the nation of my Fuehrer." Then the captain of the smoldering hulk which so recently had been the* Graf Spee *took his service pistol and blew his brains out.* ♦♦♦

Masquerade

◆◆◆ *Neither the* Graf Spee *nor the* Emden, *in a previous war, could surreptitiously overhaul a neutral vessel while pretending to be another harmless merchantman. The lofty and distinctive conning tower of the pocket battleship could be spotted when the hull was well down over the horizon.*

But the auxiliary cruisers and "Q" ships, which the British used to such good advantage in World War I— especially against U-boats—were another matter. Freighters or passenger liners, built originally for competitive speeds, could be fully armed with guns of many calibers as well as torpedo tubes and could hide all this armament behind false bulwarks, ventilators, or even within especially adapted lifeboats. In a matter of seconds, this sort of raider sailing incognito could rip away her disguise, hoist battle colors, and swing into action.

Count Felix von Luckner in his raiding yacht Seeadler— *"Sea Eagle"—was adept at this masquerade for the Kaiser's navy. He was to have several successors in World War II, among which the* Kormoran *was outstanding. She preyed on her enemies for almost a year and then succumbed, literally in a blaze of glory, taking with her a far more powerful and valuable foe.*

The 9,400-ton Hamburg-Amerika liner Steiermark *was yet to embark upon her maiden voyage in the East Asian trade when Hitler invaded Poland, September, 1939. With her diesel-electric propulsion and twin propellers, she could turn up to nearly seventeen knots, speed sufficient for overtaking most freighters.*

She not only held a fuel capacity for nearly a year's cruising, but also offered ideal, almost luxurious living accommodations for a wartime crew of nearly four hundred. The men could be berthed two to four in semiprivate cabins, instead of in fo'c's'les. Her strength of construction, comparable to that of a destroyer or light cruiser, permitted the mounting of a formidable main battery of guns upon her decks and superstructure—six 6-inch rifles, in her case. One of these "heavies," as a matter of fact, had been a part of the battle cruiser Seydlitz's *armament at Jutland. She also was fitted with fifteen torpedo tubes.*

Such convertibility, seemingly, was more than coincidence. The Third Reich, with its five years of saber-rattling, had not overlooked the preparations for aggressive war.

All in all, the Steiermark, *renamed* Kormoran, *was an ideal auxiliary raider, far better suited for charade than her slower, coal-burning forebears of World War I. Her skipper was a youthful, blond destroyer captain who, like fellow officers of the German Navy, had received an excellent education at the Mariene Akademie, Flensburg. Commander*

Theodor Detmers was tough, brave, fair, humorless, and born to command. With little interest in his country's politics, he endeavored to obey orders as given.

By the time fate put Detmers on course with H.M.A.S. Sydney, in November, 1941, his Kormoran *had sunk or captured in the South Atlantic and Indian Ocean ten merchant ships, representing almost 80,000 tons, including cargo. The cost of the* Kormoran *and of operating her thus had been made up many times over.*

The Australian cruiser Sydney *was the successor to her namesake of World War I, which had dispatched* Emden. *The new warship, registered at 6,830 tons, possessed a main battery of eight 6-inch guns, plus a secondary of eight 4-inch. She could drive ahead at the destroyer speed of almost thirty-three knots.*

But, like all cruisers, her awesome firepower was leavened by her thin skin, this thick enough only to "keep out the water and small fish," as the saying goes. She was designed to dodge blows, not take them. Even a 3-inch shell could quickly sink a cruiser, if it penetrated a vital spot—into a magazine or boiler room.

She was on patrol off the west coast of Australia, some four hundred miles north of Perth and westward of an anchorage known as Shark's Bay, when she came upon the Kormoran. *The German raider, which had sailed under several disguises, including that of the Japanese merchant marine, was now sporting the Netherlands flag as the* Straat Malakka.

This is Detmers' account of the ensuing trickery that lured Sydney *to her doom.* ◆◆◆

It was November 19th, 1941, a beautiful day with warm sunshine. As so often in the Indian Ocean the visibility was perfect. The wind was south-south-east, and had dropped to between Force 3 and 4 [about 12 miles per hour]. The sea had dropped too, and more or less the only movement was a medium swell from the southwest. The *Kormoran* was proceeding at medium speed on her usual sweep and gradually approaching Shark's Bay from the southwest.

At 1500 hours [3 P.M.] I checked the ship's course and decided to carry on without change until 2000 hours [8 P.M.], and then turn eastward towards Shark's Bay. After taking the usual look round in all directions I went into the mess for some coffee.

At 1555 hours the alarm bells began to ring, and a moment or two later an orderly arrived to tell me that a ship had been sighted ahead, probably a sailing vessel.

When I got to the bridge I saw a small light spot almost dead ahead. The lookout in the foretop was revising his signals all the time, because in the shimmering light at the limit of visibility the contours changed continually. Before long we could see two sailing ships, then a number of vessels, and behind them two clouds of smoke which probably came from an escort. I didn't much care for the outlook, so I turned away to port at 260° and ordered full speed ahead. Then I went onto the signal deck and looked through the sighting telescope of the gunnery control point. At first the air was quivering so in the heat that it was difficult to see anything clearly, but then a typical cruiser shape began to come clear. It was one of the three Australian cruisers of the "Perth" class, the fellows I had seen in Sydney Harbour

when the cruiser *Köln* visited there in 1933. It was exactly
1600 hours now.

Evasion was out of the question. There were three hours
until dusk at 1900 hours, but the cruiser coming up could
move at 32½ knots compared with our best speed of 18
knots, which we were unable to do any more on account of
the barnacles and so on clinging to our bottom and sides.
About the best we could manage was 16½ knots, approximately half the enemy's speed. And even if, against all like-
lihood, I managed to hold him at arms' length until dusk
that wouldn't help me much either because the nights in
these parts were light, with good visibility, which meant that
now he had sighted me he would not lose me again so easily.

No, the only thing to do was to keep to my course and
wait and see what happened; remaining alert all the time to
take advantage of any mistakes he might make and see to it
at least that I had a favourable opening position.

My one aim was thus to gain time; time in which the
enemy cruiser would come closer, if possible to within six or
eight thousand yards or so, so that when the shooting started
he would not be able to outrange me or to withdraw to ten
thousand yards and more. If I could get him near enough
my battery of six 15 cm. guns would not be so very inferior
to his eight 6-inch guns, because the advantage of modern
fire-control, which he possessed, would not mean so much at
short distances; and for all their simple, even rudimentary
fire-direction and control, my guns would be capable of
shooting it out even with his modern double turrets.

Of course, this didn't take into consideration the fact that
we were, after all, only a refitted passenger ship with thin

hull plates—and that we had 420 mines on board, which we certainly couldn't get rid of now in sight of the enemy.

We increased speed now and I dropped the foretop look-out and lowered the crow's nest in order not to awaken suspicion. I also turned to 250° and took up the most favourable shooting position available to me. I paid no further heed to the position of the sun, because the smoke sent up by the simultaneous performance of all our engines was so visible that the enemy must have seen us, even if his crow's nest were not manned. We now waited for the first sign that he had, in fact, sighted us.

Then at 1605 came a report to me on the bridge that motor No. 4 was out of action. Our top speed was therefore about fourteen knots and this I now sailed. The cruiser then turned towards us blinking "N.N.J." My Chief Signalman looked at me and shrugged his shoulders. Neither of us knew what this odd group of letters was supposed to mean, or how we were expected to answer it. As the cruiser was not far away now I did nothing; let him do something— something wrong, I hoped. For a while he continued to morse "N.N.J." and then suddenly he demanded, "What ship?"

This cheered up my Chief Signalman and his colleagues no end. At last the big fellow had asked something sensible, and he now hurried to me to know whether he should reply with our searchlight or our top lamp. My reply astonished him for a moment.

"Neither," I said, "Answer slowly and awkwardly like a real merchant-navy greenhorn—and with flag wagging. In the meantime they'll come even closer."

Morse signals would have speeded up the proceedings too much for me. I knew I had to fight him and I wanted him as close as possible to nullify all or most of his advantages; to gain time for ourselves and not give him too much time to ask awkward questions. After what must have been an irritating pause I had the signal-code pennant half hoisted, which meant: "I can see your signal, but I can't make out what is it." The cruiser came gradually closer. Her silhouette was very narrow. She was about three points to starboard now, but still at a distance of about 15,000 yards, and travelling at somewhere around 20 knots. Strong smoke development suggested that she was stoking up in all her furnaces.

After allowing a suitable time to elapse we informed her that we had now understood; and then, without any hurry, I hoisted the recognition signal of the *Straat Malakka*. My Chief Signalman Ahlbach had caught on now; he realized that I was playing for time for all I was worth; and in this he now aided and abetted me manfully. Of the four flags only three appeared at first, and when the four flags finally were unfurled they were hopelessly twisted. With that the signal was lowered to allow the flags to be cleared before they were hoisted again. How well Ahlbach did his job was confirmed by the fact that the cruiser had to signal twice to get us to clear our signal so that he could read it. They were quite unsuspicious, it appeared, and they seemed to be showing understanding and consideration for an awkward fellow not much good at signalling.

Now he knew who we were supposed to be: a Dutchman, the *Straat Malakka*. But would he believe it? I knew that the real *Straat Malakka* was about our size and shape, and it was certainly quite possible to take us for her. And we also knew that she was somewhere around in the Indian Ocean; but where exactly was another matter. It was to be hoped that this fellow didn't know either. By bad luck he might have left the *Straat Malakka* behind in port. Or he might inquire by wireless; but at least he wasn't doing that, for my W/T room reported that the enemy was maintaining wireless silence.

The cruiser now morsed that he had understood us at last and asked where we were bound for. Trusting to luck I replied "Batavia." This was quite reasonable, and the fact that we were now steering 250° (west) could readily be interpreted as a normal evasive course on sighting a cruiser. But what I didn't understand was why he didn't signal me to heave to. That would have been very disagreeable, because a ship losing way would have been swung round in the swell and we should have shown our broadside to the enemy approaching us in line. I took it that the British did not usually stop ships at sea unless there was something suspicious about them—for they certainly had sufficient experience in stopping and searching ships. Which could only mean that they found nothing suspicious about us. Splendid!

At 1635 hours a message arrived on the bridge to the effect that No. 4 motor had been temporarily patched up and could run again minus one cylinder. The lads had worked like Trojans to achieve that. But I kept to the same speed of 14 knots now in order not to awaken suspicions in the mind of my trustful enemy by any chance. Further, the speed of 14 knots was more appropriate to my disguise as Dutchman.

The enemy cruiser was between eight and nine thousand yards off, and still coming closer. Up to now we had ranged him with our 3 m. apparatus, but even with every precaution I thought it dangerous to let our range-finding apparatus be seen above the camouflage, so we withdrew it and used our much less noticeable 0.75 m. anti-aircraft apparatus instead. This apparatus was portable and could be used from the bridge without attracting attention. The enemy cruiser was now coming within the range that I considered suitable for my guns, and she was already so close that through our glasses we could see every detail clearly. In particular we could see that her four double turrets with their 6-inch guns and also the port torpedo-tube battery were all directed at us. As far as I could make out her eight 4-inch anti-aircraft guns were not manned. So much the better. We knew that generally speaking the British did not man their anti-aircraft guns when there was no air alert. If they had done so now it would have increased the enemy cruiser's artillery superiority.

There was no sign of any diminution of speed on the enemy's part, and she came up steadily with an unchanging bow wave, still showing us the narrowest possible silhouette. She was obviously still curious about us, and now she wanted to know what cargo we were carrying. I replied vaguely "piece-goods." They could make what they liked of that. My signalmen were working away slowly and inefficiently, and it was terribly difficult for us to make ourselves understood. I now hoisted the Dutch flag and to make the confusion still worse I began to use my wireless, sending out the "Q" signal: "QQQ *Straat Malakka*," and informing the world that we were being challenged by an unknown cruiser. Perth wireless station picked up my signals, acknowledged receipt, and gave the "understood" sign, telling me to keep in touch.

My men had been at action stations for over an hour now and it seemed a long time to wait, particularly as they could see and hear nothing; and as I expected action to be opened at any moment I now spoke to all stations over the intercom informing them that we were about to go into action with a small cruiser which we should be well able to dispose of. An answering cheer told me that everything was in order.

I could see that the enemy cruiser now had a plane on the catapult. The engine was probably warming up. At any moment it would be catapulted into the air; and once the observer spotted us from above he would recognize us at once for what we were, an auxiliary cruiser. Or at the very least he would wireless back that we looked highly suspicious. It might be possible to conceal the range-finding crew with their apparatus before the plane arrived, but the camouflage of the guns in Hatches 2 and 4 was not so perfect that it could stand such close scrutiny. The plane was almost certain to start; the wind and weather conditions simply called for it.

But at least the enemy was only something over three thousand yards away now, a beautiful shooting range. Would she slow down? Would she order us to heave to?

Would she turn her broadside on us? And what should I do? Had the time come to de-camouflage and run up the war flag? Was the enemy in the best possible position for me to open fire? No, not yet, I decided, because three thousand yards was about the extreme effective range for my anti-aircraft guns; and I wanted to bring every gun I had to bear at its maximum effectiveness in order to give me the biggest possible chance. So let her come a bit closer still. The closer she came the better it would be for us. I therefore continued to leave the initiative to the enemy.

For some time now we had been expecting a signal that would call our bluff, but so far nothing had come beyond almost casual queries which we had no difficulty in answering with some show of reason. The enemy now changed course a point or two to starboard so that the cruiser's silhouette became a little broader, which was also to the good. But at the same time she morsed:

"Give your secret call!"

We had been expecting some such signal for about an hour. There it was at last. The denouement was very close now, because, of course, we did not know the secret call sign of the *Straat Malakka*.

But for the moment I was still interested in stringing the enemy along, because every passing minute was improving my position. "Slowly! Slowly!" I called to Ahlbach, who was still deliberately fumbling with the signal flags, and dragging out matters as long as possible. The cruiser now repeated her Morse signal:

"Give your secret call!"

So much time had now been gained that she was broadside on and sailing a course parallel to that of the *Kormoran* at a reduced speed.

The range was only about a thousand yards now and we could see the cruiser's pantrymen in their white coats lining the rails to have a look at the supposed Dutchman. It was the sort of happy picture you see on a sunny day in peacetime when two ships meet at sea.

In reply to the cruiser's signal demanding that I should give my secret call I could still have done what I would certainly have done had she asked me earlier on. I could pretend to be mistrustful, and instead of replying I could have asked the cruiser her name. Had I done so I am quite certain that I would have gained further time, because that was just the suspicious sort of attitude a cautious Dutch sea captain might have been expected to adopt in such circumstances.

But the situation was different now. I needed no more time. My eyes were glued to the bearings compass, and as soon as I saw that the enemy had come practically to a standstill I gave the order: "De-camouflage!"

The time was exactly 1730 hours. The Dutch flag was hauled down, and the German naval war flag ran up and fluttered proudly in the breeze from our foretop.

As soon as my Chief Signalman reported, "War flag flying," I gave the order to open fire both to my gunners and torpedo batteries.

From the moment the order to de-camouflage was given the miracle of speed and efficiency which my men had been preparing for and practising for months took place. The ship's rails folded down, the heavy camouflage covers fore and aft were whisked away. Hatches 2 and 4 opened up to reveal their guns, the 2 cm. anti-aircraft guns were raised, the torpedo flaps opened, and all barrels and torpedo tubes swung onto the target.

Within six seconds of the order to de-camouflage the first shot was fired from our leading gun. Four seconds later the other three went into action, scoring direct hits on the enemy's bridge and in his artillery control post.

Immediately afterwards the enemy opened fire too, with a full salvo. But it roared away harmlessly over us, probably over our stern. Then we fired eight salvos, with six seconds between each salvo, without any answering fire at all from the enemy. Obviously his artillery control centre had been put out of action by our very first salvo. At that short range every shell we fired was a direct hit. At the same time our anti-aircraft guns peppered the enemy's upper deck and his torpedo batteries, and our army 3.7 anti-aircraft gun pumped shells into his bridge.

Our own torpedoes were discharged at the enemy, and to do this I had to turn to 260°, which I did with very little helm movement in order not to disturb our gunners. One of the first two torpedoes passed across the cruiser's bows, but the other hit her abaft Turret A.

An enormous column of water shot into the air and her stern dipped into the water up to the flagstaff. Both fore turrets seemed to be out of action, for we didn't get another shot from them. After we had fired eight salvos, Turrets C and D began to fire independently. Turret D fired two or three salvos, but they all went wide. After that it ceased firing altogether. But Turret C continued to fire, and with considerable accuracy. The first salvo was too high, and it ripped through our funnel at about bridge height, but its next hit us amidships and set our engine-room on fire.

Our own guns were continuing to fire rapidly and steadily and doing the enemy a tremendous amount of damage. A motor-cutter was hanging helplessly halfway over the side, the heavy turret deck of Turret B had been lifted out of its emplacement and hurled overboard.

The plane which had been on the catapult had been blown into the sea, and flames were shooting up everywhere. Not a man could show his face on the upper deck, because the fire of our 2 cm. anti-aircraft guns and our heavy machine guns was so intense, whilst our 3.7 cm. anti-aircraft gun continued to pump shells into the bridge structure.

Not a torpedo was fired at us. In all probability the hail of shells from our anti-aircraft weapons was so intense that no one could release the safety catch on the tubes.

The enemy cruiser now turned towards us and passed behind our stern. It looked almost as though she were trying to ram us, but for that she was already too far down by the stern, and she no longer had any speed. I thought perhaps she was turning in order to bring her starboard torpedo tubes into action after having released the safety catches of the tubes under cover of her lee. But no torpedoes were discharged, and our anti-aircraft guns now swept her starboard side devastatingly.

As the battered cruiser came behind our stern she enjoyed a short respite, because on account of our midships structure our forward guns were temporarily unsighted, so that for a while we had only two guns in action. I kept to my course in order to show the narrowest possible silhouette to any torpedo attack, but none came.

A lot of smoke was now drifting away to stern out to starboard from the fire in our engine-room. In consequence my gunnery officer at our artillery control point could no longer see a thing, and handed over to the anti-aircraft gunnery officer who was aft on the poop. He continued to direct the fire of our stern guns, but he was getting no counter-fire at all now, and all the enemy's turrets seemed out of action, and their gun barrels were pointing helplessly away. The enemy's anti-aircraft guns had not been manned at all during the engagement, and they were still silent.

The crews of our guns, 1, 3 and 4 used this enforced pause in their operations to cool down their barrels with fire hoses, because the rapid firing had made them so hot that they could hardly be used any longer. But it was only a short pause and then all four guns were in action again; that is to say, guns No. 2, 3, 4 and 6. Guns No. 1 and 5 were now in our firing lee and unable to take part in the further action. My gunnery officer took over again.

At about 1800 hours I wanted to turn to port to run parallel with the enemy and finally destroy her, and the helm was already in position when the sailor at the engine-room telegraph reported that the revolutions of both machines were falling away rapidly and that contact with the engine-room had been broken. At that moment I saw the wake of four torpedoes the enemy had discharged at us, but to my relief it was clear that at our present speed and on our present course they were going to pass harmlessly astern. I therefore made no change in my course and they disappeared behind us at a distance of between one hundred and two hundred yards.

Immediately after they had passed the whole ship shuddered from stem to stern owing to the failure of our engines. Shortly before this I had given instructions to be passed to my Chief leaving it to his discretion to abandon his control stand—which was cut off from the engine-room by glass—if the heat he was complaining of increased intolerably. The orderly now returned and reported that he could get no answer from anyone. The engine-room itself was out of action.

In the meantime our guns were keeping up their devastating fire and the enemy was receiving one direct hit after the other. From the fore bridge to the stern mast the cruiser was now a mass of flame and she was moving forward only very slowly. We were unable to move at all, so we sent a torpedo after her at about 8,000 yards, but it passed harmlessly behind her stern.

At 1825 hours I gave the order to cease fire. By this time the enemy cruiser was over ten thousand yards distant; drifting rather than sailing, and little more than a flaming hulk. It was growing dark rapidly now, and she gradually faded into the darkness, apparently making for Perth.

Up until 2100 hours we could see the glow, and then we saw the flames suddenly dart up even higher as though from an explosion, and after that the battered hulk of our enemy disappeared into the night.

My aim now was to lower and launch as many of our boats as were still serviceable, and now that the engagement was over I wanted to see whether it was possible to keep my ship afloat or not. Amidships the *Kormoran* was well alight, and I hurried through the corridor on the port side, and saw that the cabins there were burning. I opened the midships door into the engine-room, but billows of thick smoke rolled out, and darting flames shot up.

With some difficulty I got the door closed again, and then I hurried aft to the upper deck where I met technical personnel, who informed me that the fire-fighting equipment in the engine-room had apparently been destroyed and that the whole starboard foam equipment was also out of action. An attempt to get it into action from the screw machine chamber, which was quite undamaged, failed. There was no pressure in the damaged pipes.

In this hopeless situation it was obviously impossible to get the engine-room running again even in part, so we concentrated our efforts on trying to rescue our comrades who were shut in there, but unfortunately everything we tried failed. We were beaten back by smoke, flames and heat wherever we attempted to force a way through.

I was faced with the most difficult decision of my life now. I could probably have put out the fire in the engine-room, if necessary, by opening the floor valves in there, which could be operated from the upper deck, but what good would that have done? Whatever generators, electric motors and cable work had not suffered from the fire would have been put out of action for good by the flooding sea water. Our Power Room No. 2 was quite undamaged, and if we had had a motor there of the size of those which provided our driving power it would have been worth while to try to get the ship moving again with it, but we hadn't.

And the idea of getting her into some neutral port, limping along perhaps under improvised sails, was out of the question, because all the coasts around the Indian Ocean, and all the islands, were more or less in possession of the enemy. No, there was nothing for it—I had to make up my mind to sink the gallant *Kormoran*.

Once I had taken this decision my only job was to save as many men as I could. I might have tried to get rid of the mines, but to do so would have taken up too much time and required too many hands, so I left them where they were— they would at least make certain that the destruction of the *Kormoran* was a real job. I told off a party to watch the mine deck and report to me currently on the state of the temperature there. I hoped to have a few hours before the fire came too close to the mines to allow anyone to remain on board.

Another point was that as long as the ship was still afloat I could man the four guns of one battery in case another enemy happened to come up with us, perhaps attracted by the light of the flames in the increasing darkness. And for one thing, I didn't know whether the enemy had succeeded in sending off a wireless signal, though we had certainly heard nothing. Obviously, though, if he could he would report our position on his way back to port and thus send other ships after us.

The question of life-boats was a bit of a problem too. Two motor-boats and a cutter were too damaged to float, and only one cutter was still seaworthy. But on deck there were four of the boats in which the crews of various ships had come aboard, and fortunately they had not been dam-

aged. And in addition there were four inflatable rubber din-
ghies and a number of small rescue rafts which were lashed
down in various places over the ship's decks. All our rescue
boats were now launched and manned.

With the fall of darkness the wind had risen and was now
blowing at Force 5 or 6. The boats were straining at the lines
that still held them to the ship, and the first rubber dinghy
we had manned tore itself away and floated off into the
darkness, which was particularly unfortunate because it was
carrying mostly wounded men. A little later two of the men
who had been in it swam back to the ship and reported that
it had capsized with the loss of forty men. Unfortunately we
had been unable to help them.

At 2100 hours the boats put off, and in the meantime I
had all the remaining men piped together on the fore deck,
and 120 men and almost all my officers assembled for the
last time on board the *Kormoran*. There were two boats
available for them in Hatch No. 1, but it wasn't easy to
launch them. We had no power available and the hatch
cover had to be removed manually. The derrick proved to
be unusable and the boats had to be hauled out manually
with rope tackle, which was very hard work; but at last it
was done, and at 2330 they were both safely launched, and
the first of them pulled away.

My fire-watching group now reported that matters were
rapidly getting worse on the mine deck, with particularly
intense smoke development. Whilst the last men forward
were hurriedly gathering a few things together for what
might prove to be a very long voyage in the open boats, my
explosives officer now used his skill on the *Kormoran* her-

self, placing his charges by one of the oil bunkers. As the reports from the mine deck were growing more urgent, I gave the order to abandon ship, took charge of our war flag, and was the last to leave my ship. It was just midnight.

There were sixty-two men in my boat and only three oars, but we got away from the neighborhood of the *Kormoran* as quickly as we could. At 0010 hours precisely the explosives charge went up whilst we were still under her bows but on the lee side from the charge so that we came to no harm. I had four men pulling and pushing on each oar now and they sweated and strained for dear life to get as far away as we could before the mines went up.

At 0035 there was a tremendous explosion and the whole stern and midships of the vessel turned into one gigantic sheet of flame which shot into the air perhaps a thousand feet high. And a little after that a shower of small debris fell all around us. Even at that time we were only about a thousand feet away, but fortunately we again came to no harm. When the vast flame had died the *Kormoran* lifted her bows into the air and slipped backwards under the surface.

And that was the end of the gallant ship we had worked and fought so successfully.

> —*The Raider Kormoran,* by Theodor Detmers,
> William Kimber & Co. Ltd., London, 1959

◆◆◆ *All six hundred and forty-four aboard the* Sydney *perished. Detmers, who had lost eighty out of his four-hundred-man crew in the blistering engagement, spent the remainder of the war in an Australian prison camp. Repatriated in*

February, 1947, he was to note, "There was never at any time the slightest suggestion that I was to be brought before a court-martial, so obviously my conduct had been accepted as within the laws of naval warfare." Today, he wears the Iron Cross and the Knight's Cross. ◆◆◆

"Like the Lady She Always Was"

◆◆◆ *Less than three weeks after the destruction of the* Sydney *and the* Kormoran, *war came to the United States— on December 7 with the bombing by the Japanese of Pearl Harbor in the Hawaiian Islands.*

Staggering from the blow Tokyo had hoped would be mortal, the United States Navy suffered further losses—including the U.S.S. Houston, *one of President Roosevelt's favorite cruisers—in the Battle of the Java Sea, late in February, 1942. In fact, along with Australian and Dutch cruisers and destroyers, an entire squadron sank in that disastrous engagement.*

In April, General William H. "Billy" Doolittle's Tokyo bombing raid more than compensated in its boost to home morale for what it might have lacked in military impact. Also under way this month and continuing into May was an operation not so spectacular but of far-reaching implications —one conducted in the wide Coral Sea area by a task force built around the carriers Lexington *and* Yorktown. *This*

180

lovely, calm body of water is sheltered by the Great Barrier Reef, the Solomons, New Caledonia, and the Hebrides.

Raids against enemy shipping, as well as bases in New Guinea and the Solomons, by planes from the two carriers were climaxed by their sinking of the Shoho. *It was Japan's first carrier loss.*

In these shimmering, story-book waters, the "Lex" would add luster to a nation's naval lore. The 45,000-ton carrier was one of the most famous and prized men-of-war. She could hangar one hundred aircraft, accommodate a crew of 2,700, and hammer along at cruiser speed—the equivalent of almost thirty-eight land miles an hour.

She had been in service for fourteen years when overtaken by war. Her commanding officer when she sailed from Pearl Harbor for the last time was Captain Frederick W. "Ted" Sherman, class of 1910 at the Naval Academy and a champion boxer. This is his account of his huge charge's gallant fight for survival that Friday, May 8, 1942, as one hundred Japanese bombers and torpedo planes screamed in to the attack: ◆◆◆

The air fighting now became a melee. Our own planes were mixed in with the enemy and the sky was black with flak bursts. The Japanese spent no time in maneuvering, but dived straight in for the kill. The huge *Lexington* dwarfed the other ships in the formation and bore the brunt of the attack.

It was beautifully coordinated. From my bridge I saw bombers roaring down in steep dives from many points in the sky, and torpedo planes coming in on both bows almost simultaneously. There was nothing I could do about the bombers, but I could do something to avoid the torpedoes.

As I saw a bomb leave one of the planes, it seemed to be coming straight for where I stood on the bridge. Had I better duck behind the thin armored shield? If it had my name on it, I thought, there was no use dodging, and if not, there was no need to worry. At any rate, I had work to do to try to evade the torpedoes.

The ideal way to drop torpedoes was for groups of planes to let go simultaneously on both bows. In this method, if the target ship turned toward one group to parallel its torpedoes, it presented its broadside to the other. The timing was vital. The enormous *Lexington* was very slow in turning. It took 30 to 40 seconds just to put the rudder hard over. When she did start to turn, she moved majestically and ponderously in a large circle.

As I saw the enemy torpedo planes coming in on both bows, it seemed to me that those to port were closer than those to starboard. They were approaching in steep glides, faster than we considered practicable for torpedo dropping. The air was full of antiaircraft bursts and the din was terrific. When the planes to port were about 1,000 yards away, I motioned to the helmsman, Chief Quartermaster McKenzie, for hard left rudder. It seemed an eternity before the bow started to turn, just as the enemy planes started disgorging their fish.

The water in all directions seemed full of torpedo wakes. Bombs were also dropping all around us. Great geysers of water from near misses were going up higher than our masts, and occasionally the ship shuddered from the explosions of the ones that hit.

In less than a minute, the first torpedoes had passed astern. We quickly shifted rudder to head for the second group of planes. These split up to fire on both bows, the hardest maneuver for us to counter. Then it became a matter of wriggling and twisting as best we could to avoid the deadly weapons heading our way. I remember seeing two wakes coming straight for our port beam, and there was nothing I could do about them. The wakes approached the ship's side, and I braced myself for the explosion. Nothing happened. I rushed to the starboard bridge, and there were the wakes emerging from that side. The torpedoes were running too deep and had passed completely under the ship.

My air officer on the bridge was Commander Herbert S. Duckworth. "Don't change course, captain!" he exclaimed. "There's a torpedo on each side of us running parallel!" We held our course with a torpedo 50 yards on either beam and both finally disappeared without hitting.

Enemy planes were being shot down right and left, and the water around us was dotted with the towering flames of their burning carcasses. One plane turned upside down as it hit the water, its torpedo still slung on its belly. Before it sank, we noticed a peculiar wooden framework around the missile's nose and propeller mechanism. This explained why the Japanese were able to drop their torpedoes at such high speeds and altitudes. The cushioning devices permitted them to enter the water without excessive shock to the delicate machinery. It was a scheme still undeveloped by our ordnance experts, and gave the Japanese at least a temporary superiority in torpedo warfare.

Five bombs had landed on the *Lexington*. Two torpedoes exploded against our port side. The water spouts of three near misses which splashed water on the deck were also thought at first to be from torpedoes, but subsequent examination showed only two actual hits by this weapon.

One bomb had hit the port gun gallery just outside the admiral's cabin. It wiped out most of the gun crews in that vicinity, and started fires. In addition, it killed Commander Walter W. Gilmore, our paymaster, and Commander Wadsworth Trojalkowski, our dentist, who were in the passageway just inboard, and communications men in an adjacent room.

Bombs started fires in other parts of the ship, but none was especially serious. Fragments killed men in one of the fire-control stations aloft. One bomb passed between the bridge and the funnel and severed the wire pull on the siren, setting it off to add its sorrowful wail to the ear-shattering din.

Suddenly all was quiet again. It was as though some hidden director had signaled for silence. The Japanese planes were no longer in sight, the guns had stopped shooting for lack of targets. The sea was still dotted with burning planes; our own aircraft were seen in the distance, assembling to be ready for further action. But the enemy were through.

I looked at my watch. The entire attack had lasted just nine minutes. It seemed hours since we had first sighted the enemy planes.

Off in the distance to the southeastward, we could see the *Yorktown,* a column of black smoke rising from her flight deck. Evidently she too had been damaged. She had been attacked by both torpedo planes and dive bombers, but with her greater maneuverability had managed to evade all torpedoes and was hit only by one large bomb, which had penetrated the flight deck and exploded in a storeroom down below. It had killed 37 men outright and wounded many others. Near misses had caused several fragment holes in the hull along the water line. Otherwise the *Yorktown* was undamaged.

Taking stock on the *Lexington,* we found things not so bad as they might have been. The small fires down below were being fought by the damage-control parties, who reported that they would soon have them under control. No smoke from the flames was showing above decks. The ship had taken only a seven-degree list from the torpedo hits, and this was rapidly being corrected by shifting water ballast. The engine room reported full power and speed available if I wanted it. Our flight deck was intact. We felt like throwing out our chests at our condition after the attack. But our satisfaction was soon to be changed to apprehension.

We proceeded to land our planes which were in the vicinity, and out of ammunition or gas after their air battles. We replenished the ammunition of our guns and refilled the ammunition hoists to be ready for another attack should one come. Lieutenant Commander H. R. ("Pop") Healy, our damage control officer, was down in central station, below the armored deck, where directions for all damage control were issued and reports received. He had just phoned the bridge to inform me that all damage was under control. "If we have another attack," he said, "I'd like to take it on the starboard side, since both torpedo hits were to port."

At 12:47, the *Lexington* was suddenly shaken by a terrific internal explosion which seemed to come from the bottom of the ship. It rocked the huge structure more violently than had anything we had received during the battle. Smoke began emerging from around the edges of the elevator on the flight deck.

We called central station on the telephone but found the connection broken. The rudder indicator on the bridge was also out. All telephones were dead except a sound-powered one to the engine room. However, reports of huge fires breaking out in the vicinity of central station were soon received. The station itself was an inferno. A few men had escaped from it; others were rescued by volunteers who risked their lives in the flames, but the majority, including Healy, had been killed outright by the terrific explosion. Its cause was later established as the insidious accumulation of gasoline vapor, leaking unsuspected from our gasoline storage tanks, which had been weakened by the torpedo hits. It was an unexpected blow, but as yet we had no idea that it was to cost us the ship.

Raging fires, fed by gasoline, broke out from ruptured vents and risers. The water main was broken in the area of the explosion, making the work of combating the flames extremely difficult. Long hoses had to be led from the far after part of the ship, and only very low water pressure could be maintained. It was a losing battle from the beginning, but we did not know it then. We fully expected to save the carrier.

I remained on the bridge to direct the handling of the ship and to receive reports. Commander Morton T. Seligman, the executive officer, was everywhere, advising and encouraging the fire fighters. Small explosions of ammunition were occurring frequently in the vicinity of the fires, and Seligman was more than once blown like a cork out of a bottle from watertight doors through which he was passing. He brought to the bridge frequent reports of conditions down below.

All lights were out and the damage-control men toiled in complete darkness except for hand flashlights. The decks where they were working would grow hot from fires on the decks beneath.

Despite the loss of our rudder indicator on the bridge, we were able to steer from there for a while. It was during this period that we landed the torpedo squadron which returned so late and which we had feared was lost. Then the electric steering gear went completely out and we had to steer by maneuvering the engines, giving orders to the engine room over the one telephone still working. We were unable to use the hand steering in the station below for lack of communications to give the steersman there his course.

The fire continued to spread. More frequent explosions were occurring, and the surface of the elevator in the flight deck was beginning to glow a dull red. A report came from the engine control room that the forward engine-room bulkhead was getting white hot, and that the temperature in that vicinity had risen to 160 degrees. They asked permission, which I promptly granted, to abandon the forward engine room and use only the after engine-room space.

Then the one telephone began to get weaker. It was apparent that it was only a matter of time until it would go out completely. When it did, I realized, there would be no way of getting the men out of the engine rooms. Unless I ordered them to leave, they would stay there, trapped by fire all around them, and hemmed in by red-hot bulkheads, until they perished. Over the weakening phone, I ordered these men to secure the engineering plant and get up on deck. Although we were unable to hear any reply, presently the sound of steam escaping from the safety valves assured me they had received the message. Eventually all of them found their way through the encircling fires to safety on the topside.

We now had no power and the ship lay dead in the water. Without pressure on the main, we were helpless even to fight the fire. I called a destroyer alongside to send over its hoses, but the fire pumps on the small vessels in those early days were of such low capacity that only a trickle of water could be obtained from this source. It seemed outrageous that we could do nothing to put out the fire and save our ship.

At this time, about 5:00 P.M., Rear Admiral Aubrey Fitch (commanding the *Lexington* group), unperturbed and efficient, leaned over the flag bridge and told me I had better "get the boys off the ship." It was heartbreaking, but it seemed to be the only thing left to do. Reluctantly I gave the order to abandon ship. It was the hardest thing I have ever done. Nevertheless, if we could not prevent the loss of the *Lexington,* saving the lives of her crew was of utmost importance.

The officers and men were as reluctant to leave as I was. We had to order them to go. Most of the wounded were lowered to a destroyer alongside, the remainder going directly into small boats from the other ships. Some of the crew, while waiting to disembark, went below to the service store, which was not in the fire area. They filled their helmets with ice cream and stood around on the flight deck eating it. Knotted ropes were dropped over the side for the men to slide down into the water. Some of them lined up their shoes in orderly fashion on the deck before they left, as if they expected to return. There was not the slightest panic or disorder. I was proud of them.

I noticed one crowd waiting to go over the side at the port after gun gallery. As I approached to see what was delaying them, the men, led by Marine Sergeant Peyton, gave "three cheers for the captain." Their loyalty was inspiring.

Finally, just after sunset, all the crew were off. The water around the ship was black with the bobbing heads of swimmers. Small boats from our escorts, cruisers and destroyers were busy picking men out of the water and transferring them to the other ships. After making a last inspection to insure that there were no stragglers, I stood with Commander Seligman at the stern. I directed him to leave, as it was my duty and privilege to be the last one to go. He went down into the water. I stood on the great ship alone.

While I was pausing there, a tremendous explosion took place amidships by the elevator. Planes and debris of all kinds went high into the air. Ducking under the edge of the flight deck to avoid the falling pieces, I decided it was time to go, and slid down the rope to do my stint of swimming until my turn came to be picked up by the rescue boats.

It was dark when I arrived on the cruiser *Minneapolis*. The burning *Lexington* was an awe-inspiring sight. All the survivors had by then been taken out of the water and were safe on board our cruisers and destroyers. Admiral Frank Jack Fletcher, the commander of the *Yorktown* group, directed the *Phelps* to sink the *Lexington* by torpedoes. The great ship was lit up by her flames in the gathering darkness. The *Phelps* stood off and fired four torpedoes.

They hit and exploded with dull booms. The stricken vessel started getting deeper in the water, slowly going down, as if she too was reluctant to give up the battle. With her colors proudly flying and the last signal flags reading, "I am abandoning ship," still waving at the yardarm, she went under [about 8 P.M.] on an even keel, like the lady she always was. As she disappeared from sight, there was a tremendous underwater explosion from her magazines.

It was the end of the *Lexington*.

—*Combat Command,* by Frederick C. Sherman, E. P. Dutton & Co., Inc., New York, 1950

◆◆◆ *With "Lady Lex" perished twenty-three officers and one hundred and forty-nine men. To many aboard her, it was like losing one's home. The majority of the carrier's complement had been mustered for several years, a few even since her commissioning.*

Her loss, too, meant that only three carriers fit for action remained afloat in the whole, broad Pacific. The Yorktown would have to steam back to Pearl Harbor for repairs.

The Battle of Midway, the David and Goliath clash at Midway Island, which presaged the defeat of Japan, was but a month distant. But the importance of Midway has possibly been overemphasized by historians. There had been no naval challenge to Tokyo until the fateful Battle of the Coral Sea. Then for the first time the Imperial war lords had reason to pause and think. With what little the U.S. Navy could man in the Pacific, it had struck back hard, smashed the enemy on land, and sunk several warships and transports with their supply train in the Solomons, New Guinea, and the Coral Sea.

More than three years of unremitting struggle across the Pacific lay ahead, but as any Navy man could now say, in the words of an illustrious forbear:

"I have only begun to fight!" ◆◆◆